Salesio Mbogo Kiura

Resonance Facilitating Steps in Power Intensive Contexts

AF099219

Salesio Mbogo Kiura

Resonance Facilitating Steps in Power Intensive Contexts

Project Establishment Experiences in the Kenyan Health Sector

Südwestdeutscher Verlag für Hochschulschriften

Impressum/Imprint (nur für Deutschland/ only for Germany)
Bibliografische Information der Deutschen Nationalbibliothek: Die Deutsche Nationalbibliothek verzeichnet diese Publikation in der Deutschen Nationalbibliografie; detaillierte bibliografische Daten sind im Internet über http://dnb.d-nb.de abrufbar.

Alle in diesem Buch genannten Marken und Produktnamen unterliegen warenzeichen-, marken- oder patentrechtlichem Schutz bzw. sind Warenzeichen oder eingetragene Warenzeichen der jeweiligen Inhaber. Die Wiedergabe von Marken, Produktnamen, Gebrauchsnamen, Handelsnamen, Warenbezeichnungen u.s.w. in diesem Werk berechtigt auch ohne besondere Kennzeichnung nicht zu der Annahme, dass solche Namen im Sinne der Warenzeichen- und Markenschutzgesetzgebung als frei zu betrachten wären und daher von jedermann benutzt werden dürften.

Verlag: Südwestdeutscher Verlag für Hochschulschriften Aktiengesellschaft & Co. KG
Dudweiler Landstr. 99, 66123 Saarbrücken, Deutschland
Telefon +49 681 37 20 271-1, Telefax +49 681 37 20 271-0
Email: info@svh-verlag.de
Zugl.: Hamburg, University of Hamburg, Diss., 2009

Herstellung in Deutschland:
Schaltungsdienst Lange o.H.G., Berlin
Books on Demand GmbH, Norderstedt
Reha GmbH, Saarbrücken
Amazon Distribution GmbH, Leipzig
ISBN: 978-3-8381-1731-7

Imprint (only for USA, GB)
Bibliographic information published by the Deutsche Nationalbibliothek: The Deutsche Nationalbibliothek lists this publication in the Deutsche Nationalbibliografie; detailed bibliographic data are available in the Internet at http://dnb.d-nb.de.

Any brand names and product names mentioned in this book are subject to trademark, brand or patent protection and are trademarks or registered trademarks of their respective holders. The use of brand names, product names, common names, trade names, product descriptions etc. even without a particular marking in this works is in no way to be construed to mean that such names may be regarded as unrestricted in respect of trademark and brand protection legislation and could thus be used by anyone.

Publisher: Südwestdeutscher Verlag für Hochschulschriften Aktiengesellschaft & Co. KG
Dudweiler Landstr. 99, 66123 Saarbrücken, Germany
Phone +49 681 37 20 271-1, Fax +49 681 37 20 271-0
Email: info@svh-verlag.de

Printed in the U.S.A.
Printed in the U.K. by (see last page)
ISBN: 978-3-8381-1731-7

Copyright © 2010 by the author and Südwestdeutscher Verlag für Hochschulschriften Aktiengesellschaft & Co. KG and licensors
All rights reserved. Saarbrücken 2010

Dedicated to my dear wife and daughter:

Rachel and Kanesa respectively

&
"My great people of Embu"

Acknowledgements:

I wish to thank the many people who in one way or another have contributed towards the completion of this thesis. Whereas I will not mention all of them, I wish to acknowledge some people and organizations as representatives of the many, whom I owe a great debt of gratitude.

I especially acknowledge the financial support I received from the Friedrich Ebert Stiftung (FES) for three years. In this same connection I am grateful to the Deutsche Gesellschaft für Technische Zusammenarbeit GmbH (GTZ) for the opportunity to anchor my research in their work context.

I will remain indebted to Professor Dr. Christiane Floyd, for all her support in the cause of my research. Prof. Floyd has not only been my supervisor but also a trusted mentor who has walked with me in the rough times of the study. Her extensive knowledge and ideas are the foundation of this research's contributions. Christiane: your selfless love and inspiration is a sure sign of love that abundantly flows from your heart. Encounters with you are opportunities of not only academic but also all-round growth. You are a wonderful person whose unreserved comments, critique and advice is unique. I find it a privilege and an honor to have been supervised by you. Thank you very much.

I wish to extend my thanks to Professor Dr. Horst Oberquelle for accepting to be a reviewer of the thesis. I am grateful to you for finding time to not only read the text as it developed but also for finding time for discussions and providing me with relevant literature that further contributed to development of my ideas. Links to colleagues working on health informatics in your department was instrumental to access a wide range of literature and broadened my perspectives further.

A third reviewer of my text has been Dr. Heike Winschiers who found time on short notice to evaluate the dissertation. I thank you for your insights and willingness to share your knowledge gained by working in a context similar to that of my research. Your work on dialogical system design across cultural boundaries provided me with a starting point in the early stages of my research. Many thanks.

I thank Professor Dr. Ingrid Schirmer for her cheer and advice. It is great to know you: an open and frank friend whose advice is founded on a strong spiritual background. Many thanks for accepting to serve as chair of the examination committee amidst your busy schedule. I very much appreciate.

I thank the Kenyan ministry of health officials in Nairobi, at the Eastern provincial headquarters and at the EPGH in Embu with whom I worked. The colleagues working for various donors in Nairobi, colleagues in health related issues at the Kenya catholic secretariat (KEC), colleagues from the Christian Health Association of Kenya (CHAK), among other colleagues.

Last but not least I acknowledge the support and encouragement from my family and friends from all over.

ABSTRACT

This research extends the existing knowledge as relates to praxis of information systems development in a specific context using methodological approaches developed in a different context. It recognizes the differences between developed and developing countries' contexts as relates to technology diffusion. Specific focus is on project establishment in a developing country context. Methodological approaches for software development that have been developed in Western countries are faced with contextual realities in developing countries that require them to focus on aspects either missing or implicitly treated in their definitions.

Drawing on experiences in the establishment of information systems projects in the Kenyan health sector, reflections are presented with the aim to enrich a participatory design model developed in Europe. The study identifies influences of power relations amongst the project stakeholders as a major influence to the success of the projects. This is related to the organizational structure and culture prevalent in the sector which poses a great challenge to the embrace of participatory design in these contexts since PD assumes a level playing ground amongst project stakeholders. Propositions for methodological enrichments are framed to socio-technical approaches specifically arguing for the support of empowerment and learning in the methodologies. To set in stage processes for empowerment and learning during project establishment, the aspect of mutual understanding amongst project stakeholders is stressed and analogously understood as achievement of resonance amongst the project stakeholders. I make four propositions that I argue if incorporated as focus of methodological approaches would facilitate achievement of resonance during project establishment. I propose that methodological approaches seeking establishment of resonance should pursue bonding, coaching, witnessing of learning and moderation.

Bonding is proposed to be achieved by aligning the project activities to the context realities through appraisal of endogenous realities of the context as seen in present and past locally experienced initiatives. This will promote establishment of relationships to the extent that project participants, irrespective of areas of expertise, positions, responsibilities, attitudes and interests feel to be sharing a common fate: the success of the project. Coaching is proposed through systematic activities that encourage participants to not only build a vision for the future realities of their work contexts but to also express and pursue these visions without reference to the hierarchical relations that promote a culture of silence. Methodological adaptations are also proposed to promote learning through conducive settings that allow for reflection and participation. This is especially through dedication of ample time in the project establishment process. I propose production of shared graphical visualizations in moderated sessions aimed at revealing and sharing diverse views from different perspectives.

By embedding these propositions in iterative and cyclic methodological approaches for project establishment, application of the propositions in subsequent projects have shown improvements in achieving mutual understanding and building consensus. The propositions form a basis for further work to especially abstract a methodical model for contextualized information systems development not only in the Kenyan context but also in a wider developing country context sharing the identified issues.

ZUSAMMENFASSUNG

Diese Forschungsarbeit erweitert bestehendes Wissen bezüglich der Praxis von Informationssystem-Entwicklung in einem spezifischen Kontext, indem es methodische Ansätze verwendet, die in einem anderen Kontext entwickelt wurden. Erkennt man die Unterschiede in den Kontexten von Entwicklungs-und entwickelten Ländern bezgl. der Verbreitung von Technologie, so liegt der spezifische Fokus diese Untersuchung auf Projektetablierung in einem Entwicklungsland. Methodische Ansätze zur Software-Entwicklung, die aus dem Westen stammen, sind in Entwicklungslaendern mit kontextuellen Realitäten konfrontiert, die den Fokus auf Aspekte lenken, die entweder ganz fehlen oder in ihrer Definition nur implizit benannt werden.

Ausgehend von Erfahrungen bei der Etablierung von Informationssystem-Projekten im Kenianischen Gesundheitssektor, möchte ich hier einige Reflektionen dieser Erfahrungen mit dem Ziel präsentieren, ein partizipatorisches Design-Modell weiterzuentwickeln, welches ursprünglich aus Europa stammt. Die Studie identifiziert Einflüsse von Machtkonstellationen zwischen den Projektpartnern als Faktoren, die den Erfolg der Projekte bestimmen. Dies bezieht sich auf die im Sektor vorherrschende Organisationsstruktur und Kultur. Es stellt in diesem Zusammenhang eine erhebliche Herausforderung für die Aufrechterhaltung eines partizpatorischen Ansatzes dar, weil PD von einem gleichen Bewegungsspielraum für alle Projektpartner ausgeht. Vorschläge zur methodischen Verbesserung werden in sozio-technische Ansätze geformt, die besonders die Unterstuetzung von Empowerment und Learning methodisch betonen. Um Stufenprozesse für Empowerment und Learning während der Projektetablierung einzuführen, wird der Aspekt des gegenseitigen Verstehens zwischen den Projektpartnern besonders hervorgehoben und wird analog verstanden als das Herstellen von Resonanz zwischen den Partnern. Ich mache vier Vorschläge, welche – so meine Behauptung – falls sie als zentrale Punkte methodischer Ansätze eingeführt werden, das Herstellen von Resonanz während der Projektetablierung fördern. Ich meine, dass sich methodische Ansätze, die die Herstellung von Resonanz zum Ziel haben, auf Bindung (Bonding), Betreuung (Coaching), Erleichterung von Lernerfolgen und Moderation erstrecken müssen. Bindung sollte dadurch erreicht werden, dass Projektaktivitäten mit vorherrschenden Realitäten abgestimmt werden, wobei es zur Überprüfung von inhärenten Realitäten kommt, wie sie im Zusammenhang laufender und vorhergegangener lokaler Initiativen zu finden sind. Dies wird die Schaffung von Beziehungen in einem Masse verbessern, dass Projekt-Teilnehmer, ungeachtet ihres Erfahrungshintergrundes, ihrer

Stellung, ihrer Verantwortung, ihrer Persönlichkeit und ihrer Interessen ein gemeinsames Ziel erpüren: den Erfolg des Projekts. Coaching sollte durch systematische Aktivitäten erfolgen, die Teilnehmer ermutigen nicht nur eine Vision für die zukünftigen Realitäten ihres Arbeitsumfeldes zu entwickeln sondern diese Visionen auch ungeachtet hierarchischer Beziehungen, die eine Kultur des Schweigens hervorbringen auszudrücken und beizubehalten. Methodische Anpassungen müssen auch vorgenommen werden, wo es darum geht, das Lernen durch förderliche Umgebungsbedingungen zu erleichtern, die Partizipation und Reflektion erlauben. Dies ist besonders einfach dadurch möglich, dass dem Projektetablierung-Prozess genügend Zeit eingeräumt wird. Ich schlage auch vor in moderierter Form gemeinsame grafische Visualisierung einzusetzen, mit dem Ziel unterschiedliche Ansichten aus verschiedenen Perspektiven aufzudecken und auszutauschen.

Diese Vorschläge, eingebettet in iterative und zyklische methodische Ansätzen zur Projektetablierung, haben in einer Reihe von Projekten Verbesserungen im gegenseitigen Verstehen und dem Herstellen von Konsens gezeigt. Die Vorschläge sollen als Basis für weitere Arbeiten dienen, darauf ausgerichtet, ein methodisches Konzept für kontextualisierte Informationssystem-Entwicklung nicht nur im Kenianischen Kontext sondern auch im weiteren Kontext von Entwicklungsländern, die ähnliche Bedingungen erweisen zu abstrahieren.

Table of Contents

1. Introduction 1

1.1. Initial experiences..1
1.1.1. Organizational power structure..3
1.1.2. Contextual disparities in ISD application 4
1.1.3. Basis concepts for contextualized information systems development 5

1.2. Scope of the study..7
1.2.1. Adopted understanding of culture 7
1.2.2. Position in software development methods 7
1.2.3. Support for communication in projects 8

1.3. Research aims and objectives..9

1.4. Research methods..10

1.5. Results 11
1.5.1. Empirical experiences...11
1.5.2. Reflections on experiences 12
1.5.3. Proposed resonance facilitating steps 13
1.5.4. Organization of the report..15

2. Project Establishment: Case Stories & Research Approaches 16

2.1. Introduction 16

2.2. The projects 17
2.2.1. Project 1: Hospital information system at Hillside provincial general hospital............18
2.2.2. Project 2: Platform for storing and sharing health sector reform documents............24
2.2.3. Project 3: Platform for collaboration between the public and faith-based health service providers........29

2.3. Methodological approaches to open up the sector "black-box" 32
2.3.1. Qualitative research approaches 33
2.3.2. Action Research..34
2.3.3. Case study...35
2.3.4. Ethnographically inspired methods 35
2.3.5. Intervention in reality 37
2.3.6. Grounded theory...38

2.4. Research activity as learning, adapting and changing the rules 40
2.4.1. From using STEPS to doing 'JAD STEPS' 40
2.4.2. Research approach overview 42

2.5. Discussion and chapter closing...43

3. Contextualized Information Systems Development 45

3.1. Context issues in information systems development 45

3.2. Socio-technical approaches during project establishment........................47

3.3. Power issues from organizational structure and culture 49
3.3.1. Organizational culture 51

ix

3.3.2.	Power distance index dimension of culture	53
3.4.	**Evolutionary approaches for empowerment and learning: CBPD and STEPS**	**57**

4. The Kenya Health Sector: Structure, Actor Networks, and Interaction-Moments during Project Establishment 59

4.1. The Kenyan Health Sector 60
  4.1.1. Broad sector players 60
  4.1.2. Public health system decision-making structures 61
  4.1.3. Sector tiers and functions 63
  4.1.4. Access to the health services 64

4.2. Mikropolis Model as an analytical tool to my work 64
  4.2.1. The Mikropolis Model 64
  4.2.2. The Mikropolis Model in this study 67

4.3. ANT as an analytical tool to my work 76
  4.3.1. Identification of Actor issues, goals and relational structures in case projects 78

4.4. Beyond obsession with power structures: interaction-moments in actor networks 81
  4.4.1. Symbiotic relation: human activities and technical systems 82
  4.4.2. Holistic approaches traversing organizational structures to defuse power issues 83
  4.4.3. Interaction-Moments 85
  4.4.4. Summary of Interaction-Moments 91

4.5. Conclusions 92
  4.5.1. Reflections on interaction-moments 92
  4.5.2. Interaction-moments as handles to defuse power effects in projects interactions 93
  4.5.3. Benefits of taking a holistic organization structure participation 94
  4.5.4. Evaluation of using ANT as an analysis tool 96

5. Critical Reflections from Project Experiences 97

5.1. A culture of intensive power relations supported by the organization structure 97

5.2. Non participative nature of work with limited empowerment and democracy at workplace 100

5.3. Non existence of an information culture depicted by weak support for communication 101

5.4. Constrained opportunities for learning and technical exposure 103

5.5. Methodical responses in response to the issues 103
  5.5.1. Appreciation of informal consultations 104
  5.5.2. Identification of specific focus in interactions 105
  5.5.3. Coaching and lobbying initiatives 105

6. Facilitating Resonance in Project Establishment 107

6.1. The premise 107

6.2. Model Adaptation – First experiences 108
  6.2.1. The use of JAD in STEPS 108
  6.2.2. Proposition of using JAD & STEPS for project establishment 110
  6.2.3. Evaluation of this approach 111

6.3. A new orientation 111

	6.3.1. Pointer to major issues in the context	111
	6.3.2. Resonance metaphor for PD communication	113
6.4.	**Resonance facilitators in PD methodological approaches**	**115**
	6.4.1. Aligning to what is familiar (for bonding)	116
	6.4.2. Embracing a coaching orientation	118
	6.4.3. Dedicating ample time (to witness learning)	119
	6.4.4. Using shared visualizations (based on moderation)	121
6.5.	**Implications**	**123**
	6.5.1. Concrete implications to project establishment results	123
	6.5.2. Fit into a cyclic and iterative process	124
	6.5.3. Implication in contexts undergoing transformations	125
6.6.	**Conclusion and further work**	**126**
7.	**References**	**128**
8.	**Appendix I: Project 1**	**138**
9.	**Appendix II: Project 2**	**152**
10.	**Appendix III: Project 3**	**161**

Table of Figures

Figure 1: Screenshot from Project 1 results 24
Figure 2: Screenshot from project 2 results 28
Figure 3: Screenshot of results from project 3 31
Figure 4: Schematic representation of my research practice 39
Figure 5: Summary of research practice overview 42
Figure 6: Leavitt "Diamond": Components of the organization (Keen 1981 p. 25) 50
Figure 7: Major Kenya Health sector stakeholders 61
Figure 8: Structure of decision making and public health services provision in the sector 62
Figure 9: Levels of authority and decision-making (adapted from Oyaya & Rifkin 2003) 63
Figure 10: Network of facilities in the Kenya health sector 64
Figure 11: A pictorial representation of the elements of the Mikropolis platform (from Porto &Simon 2007) 66
Figure 12: The interrelation of specific organization structure and use of technology 68
Figure 13: Health sector macro perspective with indication of collaboration 69
Figure 14: Health sector micro- perspective indicating relations 70
Figure 15: Stakeholder categories and roles 72
Figure 16: Stakeholders structure 72
Figure 17: Stakeholders categories and roles 73
Figure 18: Stakeholder structure 73
Figure 19: Stakeholders categories and roles 73
Figure 20: Stakeholders relations 74
Figure 21: Project 1 actors' issues and goals 79
Figure 22: Matrix of actor power strengths 79
Figure 23: project 1 highlight of actor power relations 80
Figure 24: Static organizational arenas of project participants 85
Figure 25: Project interactions beyond the organizational arenas 86
Figure 26: Actors in interaction-moments during project 1 89
Figure 27: Actors in interaction-moments during project 2 90
Figure 28: JAD Steps (adapted from Chung et al. 2006) 108
Figure 29: Relation of the context issues and the engagement approach 124
Figure 30: Cyclic production of establishment results 125
Figure 31: Overview of project time line 143

1. Introduction

Recent literature has questioned the application of Information Systems Design Methodologies in diverse cultural backgrounds especially in relation to the application of methodological approaches originating from the Western countries in developing countries. The point of departure is that methodological approaches are sensitive to application contexts. Assumptions that are applicable in one context cannot necessarily apply to a different cultural context. Biru (2008) using experiences from software development projects in Ethiopia, argues that methodologies with origins from the West have implicit assumptions and deficiencies emerge when applied to non-Western cultural contexts. This is because the previous background assumptions no longer hold as they did in the West.

Biru (2008) suggests a new methodological approach that considers the prevalent unique characteristics of technological systems' demand and the context's specific realities that influence supply of such systems in those contexts. Winschiers (2001) on the other hand proposes a dialogical approach as a befitting technique to systems design and development across cultural backgrounds. This study takes a similar position and revolves around efforts to enrich methodological approaches for systems development in specific contexts. The study proposes a methodological approach for establishing such projects, with emphasis on project establishment stage.

1.1. Initial experiences

With background in advanced software engineering course and practical software development experiences in Germany, the researcher set out to develop a hospital Information system for "Hillside" Provincial General Hospital (HPGH) in Kenya. Besides software engineering technical knowledge and experiences, I was also armed with two worthy sets of knowledge: First, I did a background study on participatory design and development of software. This set my ambition to not only develop a functional system but also one that is acceptable at the hospital, has socio economical justification and is sustainable. A strongly inspiring work was that of Dahms and Faust-Ramos (2002) that convincingly argues for "community development from within". Secondly, I studied the STEPS methodology of Floyd et al. (1989a) and bagged STEPS as the tool to realize the system. The project model of STEPS was ideal in achieving the project's ambitions. It starts with project establishment, then system production (design, specification, realization and embedment preparation), followed by application (use and maintenance) of a system version that will be revised to inform a follow up iteration of production and application.

Once at the hospital, and having decided on developing a module for the health records and information management department, one of the initial experiences with a clinical officer went as follows:

> **We asked:** *"In your work, you have to tally the sicknesses (diagnosis) that you consult. You as well make a tally on the number of patients that you see. What do you think needs to be done to improve the accuracy of that data?"*
>
> **Participant:** *"I don't think we can do much here, we are supposed to tally diagnosed cases in the MOH 701[1] form, which we do. We don't have any problem with that although sometimes it's hard to correctly generalize sicknesses like in the MOH 701 list. The ministry should really think of how specific the information they want should be."*

From this excerpt, it is clear that the officer considers his recording tasks and responsibilities as service to the Ministry. The detachment is depicted by the belief that any improvement or a need for tools review is the Ministry's responsibility and not his. Therefore, participative collaboration with him (such as to review his tools) would only be meaningful in the event that they recognize their deductions based on daily experiences are an indispensable input in instituting change. This opened up a new insight for the project; the organizational structure in place and by large the organizational culture, defined the staff's participation and collaboration capabilities.

According to the ideals of participatory design, a system that accurately reflects the work of the clinical officers can only be designed collaboratively with the officers. They are the experts who best understand their work modalities.

---

[1] MOH 701 form refers to a form that has a list of diseases on it. The list is supposed to feature all possible diseases and diagnosis that a clinical officer or any other health official making a diagnosis is likely to encounter

However, this information together with our previous experiences indicated that participatory project establishment was not going to be a smooth venture characterized by meeting, brainstorming, aggregating the ideas, sketching the requirements (aware of concerns), agreeing on the notion of the system desired and comfortably embarking on development of a 'first prototype'.

Understanding the promises of participation is not enough to initiate collaboration. Although the users find participation appealing, the prevalent conditions such as levels of democratic space at work, empowerment and the general status quo of the organization, limit the ability to engage in participatory development. The fact that STEPS was not entirely helpful lead this study to argue for concrete methodological steps that would promote addressing the prevalent issues during project establishment.

1.1.1. Organizational power structure

During the earlier mentioned meeting that brought together the system designers and the hospital representatives, the *"Ministry"* mentioned by the clinical officer referred to the national administration offices of the Ministry of Health. All activities and operations in the health sector are defined at the national level. Certain characteristics were evident from the participants. They were exceptionally attentive, tense and rarely gave their personal contribution on issue at hand. Informally I came to learn that such meetings were recognized as instruction- giving forums. The participants attended believing that the conveners, who are usually from high up the hierarchy (Ministry Headquarters), have come to point out their mistakes, reprimand or, at best, give a new directive to the staff at the hospital. It was inconceivable that in my case it was purely a suggestion that was being sought on how to improve their work arrangements and tools.

The sector is hierarchically structured with a strict power relation that sees the authority flow down from the top national levels to the lower levels. This authority is never questioned. The organizational structures at the lower level are expected to receive directives and act upon them. This pointed out that the relations in the hierarchy are divided by strict power intensive realities.

To embrace principles of collaboration for participatory work, the methods at my disposal needed to be adopted to suit the experienced state of affairs. This study takes special interest in the power relations reality in the organization structure of the sector by explaining the contextual differences that are prevalent and consequently affect practice of participatory design. Comparisons are thus drawn to application of the same methodologies in the Western context.

Other studies have also identified power relations to influence adoption of technology in different contexts. For example Lee (2008) studied the adoption of public management information system in the Korean government. He found out that the government bureaucrats' power within the hierarchical structure, their administrative roles, their ability to use existing computer applications and their attitude toward the effects of information technologies (IT) on managerial values influenced the systems adoption. Oliver (2003) identified the power of university administrators to influence behavior as playing a critical role in the adoption of enterprise resource planning systems in selected universities. These two studies show that the power relations prevalent in organizational settings influence technology deployment. The issues and conflicts between those with power and those without can be studied in the context of participatory design methods, whose initial goal is about resolving conflicting interests in the technology adoption in organizations. *"PD began in an explicitly political context, as part of the Scandinavian workplace democracy movement"* (Ehn & Kyng 1987) The political characteristics in a context are part of the prevalent culture in project settings.

1.1.2. Contextual disparities in ISD application

In practicing PD (Participatory Design), the goal is to develop software that will be applicable and support work processes irrespective of project background. However, different contexts call for different methodologies of attempting to create a "level playing field" – one that overcomes differences in hierarchy, authority, and power so that both structure and knowledge can emerge that will enable useful, appropriate software to be built and accepted. PD methodological approaches implicitly assume that a level playing field is necessary and it's either already in place or can be easily achieved. Different opinions are held on how this level playing field can be achieved across different contexts, even across Western cultures.

For example Nyce and Bader (2002) reported that in the Scandinavian point of view, it at best requires a convincing project presentation and at worst a design and development effort. The ensuing discussion should then come to an agreement about what principles guaranteeparticipant parity and equity. On the other hand, the United States view discussion exchanges as weak (if not doubtful) forms of action. Design and development efforts privilege those who make a strong rhetorical claim about solutions, rationality and technical competence. In the United States therefore, it's the case that PD practice will orientate more to results governed by science and engineering with the notion that rules, principles and procedures are sufficient to guide human events. This contrasts the Scandinavian context where social democracy themes of equity, reason, reform and democracy are privileged.

These disparities are manifestations of cultural differences with a bearing on the constitutive history of power and culture that these contexts have. The background structures and knowledge in these contexts are opportunities to enrich the methodological approaches for PD. I argue that it is necessary to not only take the communities as the points of departure but also to marry PD projects' goals with the strengths of the contexts. The success of this can be evaluated in how far the anticipated technical solution finds alignment with the target context. This is the convergence of human and social roles in introducing and embracing technologies.

1.1.3. Basis concepts for contextualized information systems development

As Biru (2008) states in discussing the evolution of software development methods, the central themes in current methods have become organizational issues centered on such social aspects as cooperative, participative, learning orientated and adaptive working techniques. System development and methodological adaptation is to be understood as an undertaking that calls for successful networking among the project stakeholders. This comprises the users, developers and decision makers in the organization. These stakeholders bring their interests and attitudes into the engagement that ultimately gives information on how to achieve a level playing field.

While focusing on establishment of software systems design and development, I believe that successful project establishment can only be achieved in the background of mutual understanding of the problem and process to the solution. In addition, harmony amongst the stakeholders is important irrespective of context and their represented interests.

I understand that these concepts of mutual understanding and harmony resonate with the ideals of Community Based Participatory Design – CBPD (Wallerstein and Duran, 2006). The foundational tenets of CBPD are marriage of community development goals with knowledge creation that is based on a commitment to focus on and augment existing strengths and assets in a community. The community is recognized as a unit of identity. A sense of identity is cultivated through emotional connection with (other) members.

CBPD recognizes the power division in participation contexts and fosters reciprocal transfer of knowledge, skills, and experiences based on support for co-learning in the process:

> *Essential to community-based participatory and action design is the active re-allotment of power between all involved members and constituents in the (research) process. CBPD emphasizes reciprocal transfer of knowledge, skills and capacity throughout the process, imparting community members with tangible and practical benefits as a result of their engagement and participation. Thus, CBPD strengthens co-learning and capacity building among all partners (Flicker et al. 2007).*

CBPD closely follows results of its influence on oppressed people in developing countries and therefore recognizes the challenges inherent in working in a society where the powerful feel threatened (Fals-Borda 2001). In my case, the power relations are a threat to the establishment of the project. Here, CBPD finds even more relevance given that its participatory ideal is aligned with the emancipation agendas that promote the capacity to learn in a culture of silence and limited self articulation. Even in eschewed power networks, the less strong players in the network have important knowledge that can be galvanized for change by facilitating skills development that will empower them to recognize the roles they may take in changing their social conditions (Freire 1993). This is the vision I have for applying PD methodologies in cultural settings such as the developing countries.

Scope of the study

1.1.4. Adopted understanding of culture

The concept of culture in developing countries is broad. With regard to cultural influence in developing technical systems or transferring technologies to these contexts, it is necessary that specific manifestations of culture are selected. To understand the influence of culture in designing and developing IS, Cabrera et al. (2001) characterized culture into 3 categories: organizational, occupational, national cultures.

National culture is primarily based on differences in values which are acquired in early childhood from the family. *Occupational culture* are values acquired through schooling and professional training. It comprises of values and shared practices on how things should be done in the context of some occupation. *Organizational culture* is based on differences in norms and shared practices learnt in the workplace and considered valid within the boundaries of a particular organization. I identify organizational culture as the crucial cultural phenomenon that influence IS design and adoption.

I adopt the definition of organization culture as "*a pattern of basic assumptions and beliefs, developed by a given social group throughout its history of internal integration and external adaptation, that has worked reasonably well in the past to be considered by the group as valid and important enough to be passed on to new members as the correct way of interpreting the organization's reality*" (Cabrera et al. 2001). This research is anchored on those factors specific to the Kenyan health sector that have over the years come to define the players' behavior and attitudes. These are manifested in the specific characteristics they bring in moments of engagement as project partners.

1.1.5. Position in software development methods

Project design follows a systematic approach that guides the engagement as a strategy guides the operations of an organization. Whereas there are many methodologies and models used as systemic guides to design and develop software systems, the general characteristic of all methodologies is the recognition of a process from understanding the problem (requirements gathering) to developing and sustaining a technically sound solution. We take special interest in the requirements elicitation stage which Brooks (1987) has summarized as: *"The hardest single part of building a software system is deciding what to build....No other part of the work so cripples the resulting system if done wrong. No other part is more difficult to rectify later"* (Brooks 1987, p. 17).

We however step back and recognize that this elicitation must be preceded by the successful establishment of a project. We subscribe to the goals of project establishment as argued by Andersen et al. (1990) as: *analysis of prevailing conditions and their influence at the location (context) of project execution that includes clarification of the big picture of the project and setting up of a project team*. This research concentrates on the experiences at the projects establishment to enrich by way of concrete propositions the way to differently carry out the establishment process.

1.1.6. Support for communication in projects

In recognition of the target contextual environment and having identified the point of engagement in the development methodologies, it is important to be clear about the goal, specifically viewed for both the development method phase and in recognition of the context.

Christel & Kang (1992) identify the major issues of requirements gathering as i) defining the system scope ii) fostering understanding among the different communities affected by the development of a given system and iii) dealing with the volatile nature of requirements. I argue that the support for communication is the most important aspect that determines the success or failure of project engagement and therefore methodologies have a duty to support project team communication. This argument is closely linked to the results of study by Winschiers (2001).

This study identified problems encountered with transferring technology and related knowledge as the lack of common understanding by experts of the target environment, the understanding of the value systems and background attitude. The study goes ahead to propose the embrace of a dialogical engagement that has a connotation of communication. It is imperative therefore that from the three major issues in requirements elicitation, the fostering of understanding needs special attention.

Scope is defined when there is agreement on the selected extent to which the project covers within the given constraints. Volatility will be managed (or even avoided) when communication has enabled mechanisms for thrashing out issues including definition of protocols to manage changes in requirements. I propose that the ideal goal is the achievement of common mutual understanding that gives way to an engagement characterized by "meeting of understandings". Bratteteig (2003, p.1) describes the possibility of experiencing in systems development; *"the feeling of moments of perfect understanding when working together to create an artifact that neither of us could have made without the other – the feeling that we can create an artifact that will really work."*

1.2. Research aims and objectives

In this research, I demonstrate the influence of organizational power in relation to a participatory design methodology. Taking the position that the relations, as defined by organizational structures, play a role in the failure of most system development approaches when applied in different cultures, I aim at making a contribution towards the promotion of a development methodology that is sensitive to power issues in organizations. While investigating the limitations of applying a current methodology to a different culture with respect to the specific context features of the culture, I aim at enhancing the effectiveness of the methodology by proposing approaches that make explicit the implicitly assumed focus (Biru 2008, Winschiers 2001).

Resonance seeking steps underline the recognition that the project team must develop a concerted effort to achieve mutual understanding and harmony of ideas. To achieve harmony of ideas, it is necessary to devise techniques that support the narrowing of the gaps reflected in the participants' divergent levels of knowledge. I analogously understand the meeting of different positions and levels of knowledge to the achievement of physical resonance. Methodological approaches in these contexts are proposed to increase the levels of resonance amongst the represented interests. To achieve this, I seek to bring together ideas from organizational culture, political dimensions of empowerment and workplace democracy that are promoted by learning in an incremental and cyclic version at the pace of the cultural context's participants. The study merges these findings to methodological steps informed by a developing country context of intense power relations. This approach is aimed to be valid in a cultural setting exhibiting the identified issues that confronted the researcher. In general, I aim at giving practical contributions to the efforts to develop culturally aware methodologies based on our experiences in the Kenyan health sector but applicable in any other sector with the same characteristics.

1.3. Research methods

The theoretical background to this study is based on a qualitative research strategy known as "grounded theory". It involves the collection of a small amount of data and the subsequent exploration of concepts. Using grounded theory strategy means that theories are derived from the data and later applied to larger sets of data (Orlikowski 1993). This study takes an inductive approach to explore concepts based on specific data collected from a qualitative research strategy.

A specific interaction at a hospital during a three months stay at the hospital forms the basis of the initial empirical data. This case study visit seeks to primarily familiarize with the target work environment, infrastructure, processes and other logistics of project establishment as described in STEPS. Concrete approaches included workshops, individual meetings and sustained observation of the staff in their setting. Ethnography goals of developing a holistic view of a system (the health sector) are also applied especially to build relationships, seeking development of mutual understanding and establishment of common grounds with the participants. This necessitated a deeper understanding with "the way things are done there" rather than imposing a prescriptive solution to the problems. I acquired a deeper understanding of human behavior and at the same time bonded with the subjects (in my case the hospital and the other health sector players).

The theoretical sensitivity necessary in 'grounded theory' was done via in-depth study of Participatory design methods, especially the Scandinavian approach and the STEPS methodology. Also applied was my knowledge in management and representation and a solid background in software development approaches especially frameworks based development of web applications.

1.4. Results
1.4.1. Empirical experiences
The study is validated by three projects in Kenya's health sector. The first project is at a general-practice middle level hospital where a project establishment exercise was done in the course of the study. A system module for reporting morbidity and mortality from the inpatient department was developed.

Other projects were done at the national level with policy making organs in the health sector. The projects involved development of web based collaboration platforms for sharing sector documents. This was done in collaboration with an international development partner (donor agency). One of these was started as a collaboration effort between the health sector donors working in Kenya and the government's health reform secretariat with the aim of simplifying access to relevant documents by all sector stakeholders for better input in the reforms. A central reservoir of sector documents was developed, featuring simple login to upload and download documents. A second similar project brought together representative organizations of faith based health service providers (FBHS), the ministry of health and the health donor in a technical working group mandated to work out a policy for the FBHS providers to benefit from the central government's budget allocations. This project was conceptualized to form a platform to document the process and facilitate sharing results (reports, minutes of meetings, events, studies, etc).

In these projects I took an active role in the whole process that included development of project concepts and executing the projects. Having applied the STEPS methodology as a methodological approach, I took the project establishment step of the methodology and present reflections on the process that was involved. I present the specific features arising as a result of carrying out the projects in the Kenyan health sector in terms of power relations prevalent in the organization structure, attitudes and interests and relate the project establishment to negotiation between project stakeholders.

The study uses the metaphor of resonance to highlight the focus of interaction as contention of attitudes. I propose the ultimate goal is to have the project participants reach a mutual consensus in which their perspectives find harmony. The hypothesis confirmed is that when PD is applied in a developing country setup where the concepts of freedom (including freedom of expression), democratic principles at work places, forums for initiating dialogue and opportunities for learning are absent (or at least not as explicitly available as in the west) , then the focus of PD engagement approaches will change. The change is likely to involve the focus and assumptions of the methodologies.

1.4.2. Reflections on experiences

Reflecting on organizational culture, I situate my work on the processes of supporting project establishment in a collaborative approach with participating stakeholders. The observation reached was that communication is central to the engagement; however this is confronted by unique power characteristics in the health sector.

The existing methodological approaches need to be enriched by way of concrete steps that focus on overcoming barriers from the context, especially those centered on power differences in the sector. The goal is to achieve harmony of ideas and mutual understanding that is sustained by empowerment of the project stakeholders in a continued learning process.

I was confronted by three main issues:
- ***National organizational culture.*** The health sector is characterized by a hierarchical organization structure. The "followers" endorse the superiors' power, authority and influence. The interaction with the sector staff clearly exhibits this setting in their response to invitations to express their definitions of organization and workplace improvement measures.
- ***Workplace politics***. The prevalent culture does not support embracing expressiveness in making decisions that touch on the appraisal of their work settings, their work organization and priority areas. A culture of silence does not support the identification, expression and negotiation of interests, development of democratic orientations in the work and the unavoidable stakeholder empowerment in the process.
- ***Learning and technical capacity development***. There are limited opportunities for keeping abreast with what's happening technologically, limited opportunities for personal development and generally narrow technical exposure. This is a very limiting factor in

projects right from inception unless mechanisms for "capacity development" of the project stakeholders are provided. Moreover, planning concrete steps for progress that follow directly from the current know how of the project-stakeholders is not a trivial exercise.

Taking these three issues as indicators that call for PD approaches, I seek to argue for the enrichment of the STEPS methodology through proposition of concrete steps that directly address the issues raised in an engagement to participatively establish a project. In view of these issues my point is that it is not enough to embrace the ideals and concepts of PD but to also orientate its practice to recognize the issues as fundamental social factors in the context with implications at personal, interpersonal, and organizational levels. The ways that the project stakeholders are able to supersede these factors is compared to achievement of resonance amongst them. This is proposed to be achieved through a continued cyclic interplay of the steps in ways that ultimately promote attitudinal changes.

1.4.3. Proposed resonance facilitating steps

In summary, I propose the following methodological steps as highlights in the management of project establishment in the Kenyan health sector and related contexts:

a) Aligning to what is familiar
b) Embracing coaching orientation
c) Dedicating ample time
d) Using shared visualizations

a) Aligning to what is familiar. Sustained interaction forms the basis of the whole project establishment process and can be done as interviews at individual, departmental and group levels. The bulk of this interaction takes the form of ideational communication, involving exchange of propositions. A high level view of the problem is maintained with a major focus on the sought after technical solution. The users are at liberty to critique their processes and "dream" about technological and other work re-organization solutions. Technical experts on the other hand establish rapport that allows them to "comfortably guess" understanding of the organizational context and share these observations with the domain experts. In such a setting the project team members are facilitated to unlock their potential and expand their views about their work and technical know-how. Individual convictions, attitudes and beliefs are

exposed with the possibility that the users remain convinced of incorporation of their practical hard learned experiences in future solutions about their work.
b) Embracing coaching orientation. Using tools and methods familiar to the team taps on existing competencies and promotes feeling of continuity and gradual change from the present. This is a gradual process as the users identify their status quo as the point of departure for proposed changes and re-arrangements of work place structures. This promotes identity with the users, enriches contributions, engagement, and articulation in the whole process.
c) Dedicating ample time (for the process). Project participants are motivated by settings that give the feeling of freedom, feelings of emphasized understanding of presented materials and patiently offered opportunities to respond. The setting of interaction venues help to avoid disorientation from work environments in which case the users are able to give their best with the least distraction possible.
d) Using shared visualizations. Shared representations are used that although initiated by a single participant, develop into a group's creation. The differing views and perspectives are captured from the group as they extend the shared graphical representation. Active contribution and feedback that opens up the group and dilutes the strict power relations as the shared representation evolves to be a creation of the whole. Compromise and time-out periods enable building intra group rapport as a manifestation of harmony and shared resonance.

By having a repeated use of these approaches, resonance is manifested by the produced artifacts as representing the agreements on requirements and decisions that will support project continuation. It must be emphasized that it is the interactive and cyclic interplay between the project stakeholders' attitudes and these approaches that will lead the participants finding identity with each other and thereby assuming states of resonance amongst themselves and the project situation as their communication promotes understanding.

To support communication that leads to harmony of interests, ideas and attitudes that get team representation, I propose using the physical resonance metaphor as a lens to understand what needs to transpire in the project team. Physical resonance occurs when one body vibrates and another resonates picking up some of its energy. If the two bodies share close enough natural frequencies, they resonate together. Interactions in a PD informed project needs to exhibit communication whose objective is to narrow the gaps presented not only by the differing expertise domains but also specific attitudes and interests. Observations, interpretations, reflections and explanations of the project situation will be picked up and amplified by others leading to successful project establishment.

1.4.4. Organization of the report

The general organization of this thesis is as follows. In the next chapter I introduce the projects I have selected as the basis for empirical experiences and describe in detail the research methods used. Chapter three gives a background of contextualized project establishment in information systems development. Context issues are identified and a conceptualization of how the context issues can be addressed is identified in relation to specific evolutionary approaches that promote empowerment and learning. In chapter four a detailed analysis of the Kenyan health sector is presented with the aim to bring forth the issues of power. The concept of interaction-moments is introduced as a concept for defusing power relations during project establishment engagements. Chapter five summarizes reflections from the description of the projects highlighting issues and actions that I took in response to the issues. In chapter six the results of the study are presented where resonance facilitating steps are proposed. The chapter ends with conclusion and an outlook to further related work. This is followed by a detailed list of the consulted references before presenting appendix 1 to 3 with concise descriptions of the projects' experiences.

2. Project Establishment: Case Stories & Research Approaches

2.1. Introduction

The results of this study are validated by my experiences when establishing information system projects in the Kenyan Health sector. These real life experiences provide qualitative information that forms a basis for an in-depth understanding and reflection on the implicit knowledge that is specific to the context in the sector. The presented information reveal how project establishment was done, bringing out the implicit details that must be considered for successful initiation of engagement in similar projects.

This chapter presents an overview of project case studies that help the reader understand the background of the study's empirical material. The brief descriptions of selected projects presented here are aimed at developing an insight into the situation in the project engagements at the time of the study. As a demonstration of ethical and research etiquette, the descriptions in the final write-up of this study will be anonymous.

Lessons shared from documented context-specific projects are instruments for learning and background to further develop approaches and processes of building computer based solutions in specific contexts (Biru, 2008). I see previous case studies as having the potential of providing values that form basis for sharing understanding and meaning with others in the attempt of interpreting reality.

There are reported observations that case stories experienced in the developing countries have not been widely documented. This has denied practitioners in those contexts opportunities to share best practices, lessons learnt and forums for cross-pollination of ideas based on practices that work. Documented case stories about experiences using a methodology as a tool in a developing country context are a fertile ground for developing context-aware methodologies. Such documentation will enable comparison of similar case stories based on practices with the same methodological approaches in the Western country contexts. This comparison can lead to generation of hybrid ideas that benefit practice in both contexts for both new and established practitioners with the studied methodologies.

While this chapter offers a brief background to the cases that form the basis of analysis in the following chapters, a detailed description of each project is presented in the appendices. Discussions on factors related to the success or failure of the cases as well as approaches followed in the actual conduct of the cases can be found here. Detailed discussion of the issues picked up from the cases is presented in a later chapter with reflections on how to enrich methodological approaches to address (or focus) on the identified salient issues.

The second objective of this chapter is to describe the approaches used in the projects. The descriptions aim at informing the reader about the strategies used to collect material and how learning processes were engaged in dealing with the material. Theoretical underpinnings of the reflections that lead to the reported results are presented as reflections on the approaches used to study the sector.

2.2. The projects

The first project is on a hospital information system at a general-practice middle level hospital. The hospital is located in Hillside town, approximately 120 kilometers (75 miles) northeast of Nairobi towards Mount Kenya. Hillside serves as a provincial headquarters and is also the district headquarters of Hillside District. Located on the southeastern slopes of Mount Kenya, the town of Hillside has a population of about 40,000 (as of the latest official census of 1999). Here, a project establishment exercise was done at the beginning of the study. Initial ideas for a detailed health information system were refined and a system module for reporting morbidity and mortality from the inpatient department was developed.

The other projects were done at the national level (in Nairobi) in close collaboration with policy making organs of the health sector. These projects have involved development of web-based collaboration platforms for sharing sector documents and generally facilitating collaborative work. These were done in collaboration with an international development partner (donor agency).

The initial project started as a collaboration effort between the health sector donors working in Kenya and the government's secretariat on health reforms. It was with the aim of simplifying access to relevant documents by stakeholders for better inputs in the reforms. A web-based central reservoir of sector documents was developed, featuring simple login to upload and download documents.

A second similar project was done with a Technical Working Group (TWG) that was mandated to work out a policy for the Faith Based Health Services (FBHS) providers. The aim was to establish a closer working relation with the public health service delivery systems. Members of TWG were representatives of FBHS providers, the ministry of health and the health donors. This project was conceptualized to develop a platform to document the process and facilitate sharing of results (reports, minutes of meetings, events, studies, etc).

In these two projects I took an active role in the processes of developing the project concepts, technical development work (implementation) and project management tasks.

The case stories are presented here in a consistent format that describes them in terms of the following aspects:
- How the project started
- Overall objectives of the project
- Participating stakeholders in the project
- The researcher's roles in the projects
- Project results
- Project recommendations (future plans at the time of writing this study)

2.2.1. Project 1: Hospital information system at Hillside provincial general hospital

2.2.1.1. Genesis of the project ideas

The idea to develop an integrated health information system for Hillside district in Kenya was coined by the researcher in early 2003 while in Hamburg, Germany. Based on his experiences in the health system in Hamburg, the development of the health information system was to be part of his contribution to the district's development by empowering the locals to easily access health related information. He envisioned following the model of information kiosks strategically placed in various locations in the district from where the district citizens would have access to all-round health information. A component of the system was to have modules where the medical practitioners – doctors and nurses in the health centers and dispensaries in the district – would access their own data that carries latest information about their profession. This would keep them abreast with advancements in health related information.

The goal of the exercise was extended to include seeking achievement of empowerment of the locals, socio-justification of the project, acceptance of the project and its sustainability by the users of the system. This lead to adoption of participatory methods as the most suited methodologies for carrying out the project. The researcher joined the research group of software engineering at the University of Hamburg and registered his candidacy for a PhD Program at the university based on the above ideas.

As a concrete participatory design and development methodological approach to be used, a framework for evolutionary participatory software development was selected as a tool. Expertise on the methodology was readily available at the group, the framework having been developed by the chair of the software engineering group and colleagues (Floyd et. al 1989a).

2.2.1.2. Detours to Hillside Provincial General Hospital

Armed with knowledge of participatory design methods and having read about other experiences from different parts of the world as documented especially by Dahms and Faust-Ramos (2002), Faust–Ramos (1999), Mikkelsen (1995), Mosar (1993), Mursu et al. (2000), the researcher established contacts in the district. He left Hamburg for Kenya and headed to the district where he met the earlier established contacts and discussed the ideas of the system. From the discussions, it became clear that the administrative framework that was concerned with information provision and implementation of health interventions in the district was understood as 'the hospital'. When it came to health-related matters, the locals had no relation to the administrative organs of the government at the county, municipal or even provincial administration structures. This was despite the fact that these government administrative structures had health administrative offices. Nobody expected the government administrative structures to provide health-related information.

This scenario presented the need to adjust the ideas. This meant the ideas of the project had to be aligned to the structures of the ministry of health as represented by the hospital and not by the health administrative offices in the district. The hospital that forms the backbone and the central point of access and provision of health services in the district is the Hillside Provincial General Hospital (EPGH). It acts as the referral hospital for the district and surrounding regions. Beside referral services, locals also have access to the casualty department.

At the hospital, I was advised to get a research permit before the hospital administration could officially deal with me. This was issued by the ministry headquarters based in Nairobi and both the health administrative offices at the district and the provincial offices referred me to the ministerial headquarters. With this turn of events, I realized that the research and accompanying project ideas had to be embedded in a given department in the ministry headquarters.

From studying the structure of the ministry, a possible linkage department was found to be the Health Management Information System (HMIS) department. Contacts were established with this department at headquarters. It however emerged that this department existed neither at the district health administrative offices nor at the hospital. To maintain the focus of the project as an intervention in the district, I sought contacts to a department that had representation at the hospital and other health structures at the district. The nearest shot was the department of health records and information that incidentally worked very closely with the HMIS department.

This was represented as a department at the hospital and existed in the district and provincial administrative and management offices. The research permit was secured via the health records and information department at the ministry headquarters.

With this permit, I was back at the hospital and received excellent cooperation from the hospital management and other departments, not just the health records and information department. The project idea was extensively discussed with the department representatives and a decision to limit the initial achievable aspects of the project to directly relate with the hospital operations was reached. The hospital did not have ICT systems in place. This meant that it was far fetched to plan for district level ICT systems when the nerve center of the district health operations did not have such systems in place.

The capacity for running and using the initially conceived system was basically not available at the district. The department of health records and information became the direct counterpart of the research. By now time was running out with limited progress in conceiving a concrete information system development project. I did a quick analysis of the needs at the hospital – the findings revealed that the practical first steps to a hospital information system was to involve reporting processes in the department whereby a system was needed to support the department's reporting obligations. These obligations are mainly to the ministerial headquarters (departments of HMIS and health record and information). The initial system module was agreed to be a system to report on the morbidity and mortality information for the inpatient department. The electronic process beginning after manual indexing of the discharge summaries from the inpatient departments had been done by the health records and information clerks.

Project objectives

At the hospital, the objective evolved to be one of implementing a reporting system for the health records and information department. The initial specialization being a module to report on morbidity and mortality cases in the format required by the records and the HMIS departments at headquarters. Whereas that was the project's technical objective, the researcher sought to contribute to the development of Hillside district by his inputs to better health sector management through facilitation of collection, aggregation and communication (dissemination) of information for decision making.

Project stakeholders

The stakeholders involved in the project were from the ministry headquarters, the provincial and district administrative units together with the Hillside provincial general hospital as the facility where the research was hosted. At the ministry headquarters, the representation in the project activities included: head and the deputy of the health records and information department, two senior officers from the HMIS and health records departments. These facilitated acquisition of the research permit that was required before others in the sector could collaborate in the project. They also acted as resource persons offering consultancy services in project discussions on issues pertaining to health information collection and reporting.

Representatives from the provincial and district health administrative offices were: the head and her assistant from the provincial health records office, the district medical officer of health (this is the senior most government health official in a district), the entire district health management team (DHMT) with special close collaboration with the district health records and information officer. These officers offered contributions on relevant matters in their jurisdiction, especially as all-round resource persons on how the sector runs at their levels of authority. At the hospital the project collaborated with the medical superintendent (head of the hospital), the hospital matron, the head of health records and information department, heads of other departments among them the outpatient, inpatient, pharmacy, dental, physiotherapy, orthopedic departments as well as clerks and other officers from these departments. They provided detailed information about the operations of the hospital, were closely involved in setting up the focus of the project, releasing staff for the tasks related to the project and were the hosts of the project providing detailed information about their processes including data and information requirements in their daily work.

Their work activities were studied in the project. The researcher and colleagues from the university in Hamburg acted as the development team with technical expertise in software engineering and information systems development. The supervisor was advising the process and was also the expert in the applied methodological approach of STEPS.

Researcher roles
Among other things, I was responsible for convening meetings, workshops and interviews with the project stakeholders; facilitating workshops; providing technical support to the facility, district and provincial administrative units in all matters related to information technology; preparation of reports for the hospital, especially the health records and information office;

sourcing of funds for the allowances and per diems that were paid to the participants in the workshops.

Methodologies and empirical materials

The methodologies that were used in the course of the project included: workshops, interviews with individuals and entire departments as groups, participating in carrying out the work at the department, observations and perusal/studying of documents from the department and the ministry of health in general. In the course of the project, I was able to collect empirical material from the experiences lived. These materials are recorded as: research diaries, records of frequent briefs to the supervisor, to the interviewees (after every interview I summarized the highlights of the interview), briefs to the scholarship agency, reports from the workshops, audio files of recorded interviews, personal diary and emails that were exchanged during the time of the project.

Project results

The achievement of the project was the development of a prototype that was used to generate morbidity and mortality reports from the data collected by the hospital. A screenshot of a sample generated report is shown in **Figure 1**. This prototype was used to summarize the reports from the data available at the hospital for over 4 months. However, it was stopped due to lack of continued support while the researcher was in Europe. The relocation of the head of the health records and information department from the hospital and other technical problems with the maintenance and operation of the single department computer also contributed to its end.

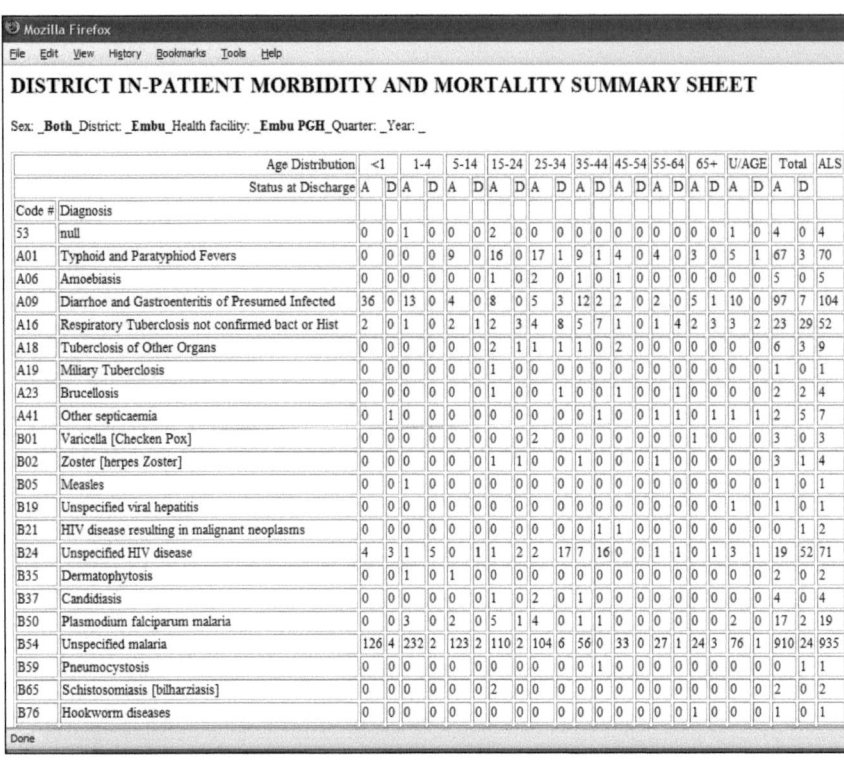

Figure 1: Screenshot from Project 1 results

Project outlook

Currently no activities in relation to the project or concrete plans for its continuation are in place.

2.2.2. Project 2: Platform for storing and sharing health sector reform documents

This project ideas fall in the context of health reforms guided by the *Paris declaration on aid effectiveness* (WorldBank 2005). The thrust of the declaration is striving for effective development assistance to developing countries by aligning the aid to the recipient countries' priorities, systems and procedures. One approach to aid efficiency is the so called Sector Wide

Approach (SWAp) which generally means the donor interventions are harmonized and aligned to the developing country's sector structures, especially its strategic plans. *"SWAps represent a 'next generation' approach to aid, and set out to provide a broad framework within which all resources in the health sector are coordinated in a coherent and well-managed way, in partnership, with recipients in the lead."* (Walt et al. 1998) SWAps typically have a joint review mechanism and performance monitoring system relying on the government's own performance assessment framework. This translates into joint planning, appraisal and development of single sector-wide operation plans in the sector with all the donors funding aspects/portions of the sector plan. Such sector-wide reforms mean that joint consultations are necessary in the work of the donors as they consult amongst themselves and with the ministry of health. It is in this context that the platform was conceived to bring together resources from the ministry of health and a group of donors working in the health sector.

The platform was conceptualized as a strategic resource that would increase transparency, facilitate easy sharing and access to such information resources in the reforms process.

The Health Donor Working Group (HDWG) initiated the ideas to implement a platform that would simplify and facilitate better access to documents from the ministry and also donor-authored documents. This began in 2005 when one member of the HDWG (from one of the United Nations health organizations) drafted a simple demonstration (in the form of a web p.) as a concept of how the members of HDWG could leverage the internet to facilitate sharing of the information. In subsequent meetings, one donor agency took up the responsibility to fund the development of the platform. It provided technical capacity, facilitated the process of coming up with detailed requirements for the project and funding the resources needed to realize the platform. The agency provided three experts, the head of the health division, the researcher and an external consultant who brought prior experiences from the governance sector.

Project objectives

The objective of the project was to develop a platform that facilitated easy sharing of documents among the HDWG members and with the ministry of health officials. The target documents were those produced by the ministry as well as those generated in the donor community. Moreover, for the donor agency, taking the lead in the development of the platform provided an opportunity to position itself as a key player in the reforms.

Project stakeholders

The project was based in the Kenya health sector at the national level where decisions on policy and guidelines are made. The project stakeholders were the HDWG and their counterparts in the sector reforms, the ministry of health. Beneficiaries included donors, international consultants, ministry officials, policy developers in other arms of the government and local population interested in information on the sectors reforms and governance policy. The HDWG provided initial concepts that set the basic requirements for the platform. Upon taking direct responsibility for the project, the donor agency did technical backstopping, advised on decisions regarding technologies and chaired the donor group's subcommittee on IT (the so-called *"website reference group"*).

Researcher roles

As an information technology expert in the donor agency, I was a resource person in the deliberations and processes that established the project. Through presentations and facilitation of technical discussions about the system in the HDWG meetings, I was involved in the development of the concept and establishment of the project together with two other colleagues from the donor agency. References from similar endeavors in Tanzania and Rwanda where the donors had formed development partners groups and developed websites that were accessible online were incorporated.

Methodologies and empirical materials

The methodologies used in the course of the project included: meetings, exchange of emails, selection of a focus group (*"website reference group"*) as well as several question and answer sessions in meetings where the researcher responded to queries and concerns from the group. Meetings of the focus group that discussed exhaustively the issues in the project can be described as adaptations of formal workshops which were fast paced to save time, given the busy schedules of the members. Prototyping approaches where demo versions of the platform were made available online in protected web directories. This allowed *"playing with"* the implementations and furnished the users with information to contribute to the project.

Emails, briefs of meetings and reports form empirical materials were used for reflection of this project's process. Others are research diaries of the researcher, calendar entries, briefs compiled after meetings, minutes of meetings and audio recording of some meetings.

Project results

The project was successful and the platform has been in use since 2006. A platform for sharing documents and other sector publications was set up. A screen- shot of the early home p. of the platform is shown below (**Figure 2**). Among other things, the platform supported functionalities to upload and download documents, shared calendar entries (including schedule of missions and other joint meetings in the sector), records of announcements, a discussion forum and a detailed description of the HDWG structures.

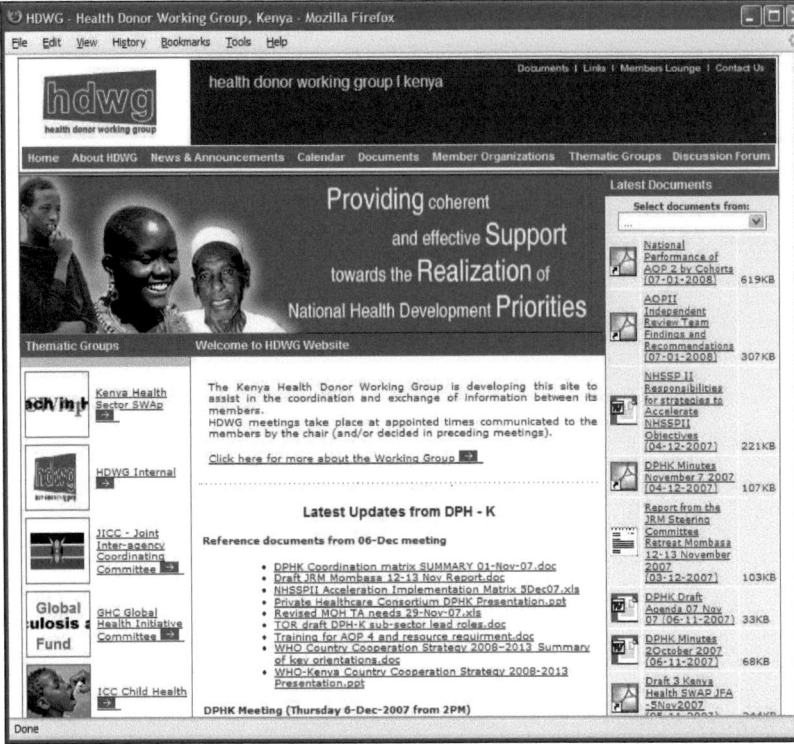

Figure 2: Screenshot from project 2 results

Project outlook

The platform is still online and continues to be further developed by the health donors group. A secretariat has been established to coordinate activities of the health donors with the platform forming a major tool for the secretariat to support coordination of the activities. It has been recognized as the best resource that comprehensively reports Kenya health sector activities. Consequently, it has been used as the main reference resource in consultancies to evaluate and appraise the sector by international consultants. The initial design has since been changed. It has integrated technologies such as web logs, an open source content management system among others. Future plans to continue the project as the one-stop resource center for the sector's documents exist. This would include: key sector management documents, policies, guidelines, study reports, operation plans, etc. The experiences have also been shared regionally in Ethiopia and Rwanda.

2.2.3. Project 3: Platform for collaboration between the public and faith-based health service providers

Establishment of this project was fast due to experiences from the previous two projects and other projects whose results are not directly reported in this study. The goal of the project comes from the context of Sector wide Approaches (SWAps) as instruments of implementing the Paris declaration on aid effectiveness and accelerating achievement of health-related Millennium Development Goals (MDGS) (UN Website) through exchange of synergies between all players in the health sector. To achieve such synergies, the engagement of the civil society as partners with the public sector is necessary.

The health-related civil society organizations play a major role in the provision of health services in Kenya. For example, a situation analysis study in the Kenyan health sector found that Faith Based Health Services (FBHS) providers cover over 26% of the facilities providing Health services (with the ratio going to over 50% of the facilities in remote areas) (MoH, 2007). In recognition to the fact that FBHS providers are key partners of the public health ministry in delivering services to Kenyans, a Technical Working Group (TWG) was formed to work out details of formalizing the partnership. One donor agency took the lead of facilitating the process through other mechanisms beyond ICT.

In this context, having established itself as a champion of information dissemination in the sector, and with the objective of sharing experiences beyond the public sector structures, the donor agency facilitated the development of a platform for documenting the process and sharing of results (reports, minutes of meetings, events, studies, etc). With a two year commitment from the donor agency to support the platform, the process commenced with a workshop of the technical working group. The researcher met them as a representative of the donor agency and facilitated a half day workshop that among other things set out the objective of the platform.

Project objectives

An observation from the technical working group was that there had been other efforts to establish partnership between the public and the civil society from as early as 1984. Approximately ten years later, the group was starting the process from scratch without any documentation from previous endeavors. A part of the objective for the platform was therefore set to provide attestation of the work from the working group. Results from the group would also be easily shared among members and other stakeholders in the sector through a central platform that would enable exchange of documents, announcements and a commonly shared calendar of events. The donor agency's position as a lead development partner in the sector was also to be strengthened together with the promotion of its achievements in capacity development.

Project stakeholders

The stakeholders in the project are as follows. The faith based organizations were represented by the protestant association, catholic secretariat and a body representing Muslims. An organization working closely with the civil society in the supply of essential drugs and other medical supplies was also represented. The ministry of health, health care financing specialists and a host of development partners completes the list of stakeholders in the project. They were all resource persons to the project on technical and programmatic areas of the working group's work on policy development, assessment of health services and mapping of facilities in the country (the key concepts of the technical working group's mandate).

Researcher roles

Among other things I was involved in this project as a technical expert in the project; advisor on technologies; manager of development and customization work; facilitator of the initial workshop and moderator of ensuing discussions in the course of the project.

Methodologies and empirical materials

The methodologies used in the course of the study included workshop, formation of a sub group of the TWG that championed the project, exchange of documents, prototyping approaches where demo versions of the platform were made available online for users to *"play with"* as the development continued. Research diary entries, emails exchanged and briefs of meetings as reports are the empirical materials that were collected for this study.

Project results

The screenshot below **(Figure 3)** shows the look and feel of the platform. The project was successfully established and has continued to be used by the TWG for sharing information about their activities and achievements. The features include functionalities to upload and download documents, shared calendar entries and records of announcements.

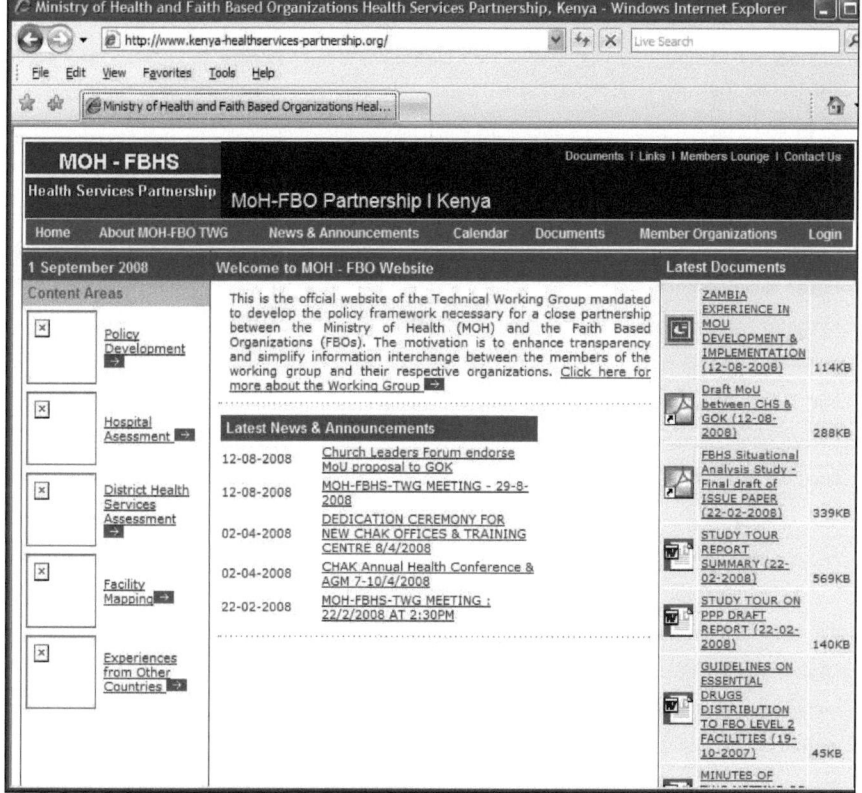

Figure 3: Screenshot of results from project 3

Project outlook

The development and operation of the platform has been successful and the chair of the technical working group is responsible for its maintenance and operation. The donor agency has plans to further develop the site to ensure the results captured in the platform remain available to the sector as envisioned.

2.3. Methodological approaches to open up the sector "black-box"

Both as an IT specialist and a consumer of the sector's services, my initial general understanding of the health sector was akin to what Latour (1987) refers to as a "black box" in his work about science. He describes black boxing as *"... the way scientific and technical work is made invisible by its own success. When a machine runs efficiently, when a matter of fact is settled, one need focus only on its inputs and outputs and not on its internal complexity. Thus, paradoxically, the more science and technology succeed the more opaque and obscure they become."*

In the same way, an outside view of the sector shows a functioning system whose internal workings are not accessible but opaque to service seekers and recipients who get the services. I present here as my research strategy the approach I used to get an internal view of the sector and how I draw conclusions from my experiences. I understand a research method as part of a toolkit (which I am generalizing as research strategy), that is available to researchers for collecting and handling research material.

In this chapter I discuss specifically a mixture of methods that can be drawn from my strategies for collecting empirical material and the approaches of thinking (as conceptual frameworks) derived from the collected material. In general, this research chose a qualitative approach (Avison & Pries-Heje 2005) through which I inductively explored concepts based on the empirical materials. Along the way, I had to make modifications to the approach of collecting the empirical material and therefore I present relationships of my approach to qualitative methods from which I draw inspirations.

My empirical experiences took place in two phases. In the first phase, I was in the health sector as an external researcher specializing in the design and development of a health (later hospital) information system backed by a development agenda for the country. Here, my approaches were aimed at establishing the information system project. In the second phase I was in the sector as an employee of a leading international development partner (donor agency) already established in the sector. In this phase, my approaches were sharpened by experiences from the first phase and successful transformation to an insider of the sector in the reflective nature guiding my adopted approaches. In the context of this employment, I have been involved in the establishment and realization of among others the two reported projects of building platforms for information aggregation and dissemination.

Research Practice

Based on the technological and sociological perspectives at the core of participatory design (PD) as a paradigm (Carroll & Rosson 2007), I can summarize my entire work as having involved two main activities: (i) presiding over the development, deployment and use of ICT technologies in a developing country (could be understood as technology transfer) and (ii) creating experiences with a methodological approach for evolutionary participatory system design (STEPS) outside its development context and hitherto application. This hybrid view of simultaneous engagement in two activities recognized the intertwined nature of taking action (work interventions) and reflectively seeking to improve the approaches (tools) for implementing information systems projects. I sought to build an understanding that would guide methodological approaches of engagement in the context as a contribution to further developing participatory design principles.

2.3.1. Qualitative research approaches

According to Myers (1997) qualitative research methods enable researchers to study social and cultural phenomena by facilitating the understanding of people and the social contexts within which they live and work. These methods assist the opening up of context "black boxes" without the risk of loosing certain context-specific details that would otherwise be lost when textual data are quantified (Avison& Pries-Heje 2005). Qualitative research approaches are therefore suited in studies that are subject to not only technological issues but also organization specific factors as my study was. Examples of qualitative methods are action research, case study research and ethnography. Qualitative data sources include observation and participant observation (fieldwork), interviews and questionnaires, documents and texts, and the researcher's impressions and reflections. Next I present the methods and sources I used in practicing qualitative research in my reported engagement.

2.3.2. Action Research

In general, action research is an approach in which the researcher participates directly in a project. The definition of action research that captures my value of using this approach is from Rapoport (1970): *"Action research aims to contribute both to the practical concerns of people in an immediate problematic situation and to the goals of social science by joint collaboration within a mutually acceptable ethical framework)"* (referenced by Avison & Pries-Heje (2005) p. 245).

This definition is appealing since it captures a major aspect of my tasks that sought to find solutions to practical issues experienced by the projects counterpart. This was, as the definition stresses, in close collaboration with the people in their actual work lives. At the hospital, reporting was a real concern that needed technical assistance to fulfill while at the sector's policy making levels, the issues of sharing (disseminating) information was not only a concern but an urgent need whose technical solution was long overdue. Avison et al. (1999) have argued that action research is an iterative process that involves researchers and practitioners encouraging the former to experiment through intervention, to reflect systematically and to modify their views as a result of the reflection.

My experience through which I drew a new understanding of the sector practitioners and their daily work processes confirms this argument. The collaboration with them called for changes in my approach especially as it exposed assumptions that I had unconsciously acquired in Europe when it comes to interacting with people in situations that necessitate criticism. The project participants understood the technical opportunities available to them and how well they fit in their context through their participation to find technical solutions. This experience is supported by the work of Hult and Lennung (1980), *"Action research simultaneously assists in practical problem solving and expands scientific knowledge, as well as enhances the competencies of the respective actors, being performed collaboratively in an immediate situation using data feedback in a cyclical process aiming at an increased understanding of a given social situation ..."*

(referenced in Cockburn 2003). As Galliers (1992) argues that one of the strengths of action research is that *"... the researcher's biases are made overt in undertaking the research"*, it was clear that from the collaborative work with the sector experts, my outlook and views on the sector were changed. A cited weakness of action research in the literature is the observation that it presents the risk of being restricted to a single project and organization causing difficulties in generalizing results. My findings however analyze results from several project experiences in the sector where different organizations and consequently different actors interacted.

2.3.3. Case study

From the earlier presented case stories, the research can be said to have taken a case study approach, viewing each of the projects as a case. Moreover, the descriptive accounts of the cases clearly indicate that this research took a similar approach. I have used the case study method in its broad understanding as an approach to study complex phenomena in its institutional context. Yin defines case study *"as an empirical inquiry that investigates a contemporary phenomenon within its real-life context, especially when the boundaries between phenomenon and context are not clearly evident"* (Yin 1994, p. 13).

Given the specific areas that my study concentrates on examining organizational and people features in the health sector, the thrust of the observations is far from being technical issues. The case stories trace the processes of grappling between context specific issues on one hand and the ideals of participation on the other as concerns choices that people are called to make in establishing information system projects in their daily complex work processes.

Given my extended periods of stay in the sector and the close association I developed with the sector, my approach has the features beyond case study method, which I understand as ethnographic inspirations.

2.3.4. Ethnographically inspired methods

Having defined the case as the Kenyan health sector and taking the approach of orientating my work towards the actions that I undertook collaboratively with the workers in the health sector, I wish to present an overview of the specific methods I used in the research.

Ethnographic research comes from the discipline of social and cultural anthropology whereby in its practice, researchers are required to immerse themselves in the life of people they study and seek to place the phenomena studied in their social and cultural context (Myers 1999). Whereas in case study the primary sources of data are interviews and documentary evidence such as annual reports, ethnography seeks deeper details in which data sources are supplemented by data collected through participant observation and participation during the field study (Avison & Pries-Heje 2005).

From the initial encounter in the sector in September 2003 where power situations played in my eyes as illustrated in the introduction, it was clear that broad cultural aspects were key factors in the study. To successfully establish a project, I needed to better understand and tame these factors. I needed an in-depth knowledge in ethnographic approaches.

Ethnography facilitates development of *an intimate familiarity with the dilemmas, frustrations, routines, relationships, and risks that are part of everyday life* (Myers 1999, p. 6). In my study, this kind of intimacy was necessary for deconstructing the context of the sector from an outsider perspective (IT specialist working in the public health sector). This resonates with the epistemological grounds of ethnography with respect to knowledge constructed in everyday activities by practitioners in the course of their complex situations.

Building an in-depth understanding of knowledge from face-to-face encounters with individuals, groups and communities called for use of what is referred in literature as *mixed methods* approach (Maxwell & Loomis 2002, Shipman 1998). The suitability of using mixed methods is the ability it gives the researcher to adapt to the needs of the context. Over time, the researcher gains multi-pronged strategies to "unwrap" the context's implicit features that are embedded in the usual and normal daily life of the studied people. Bellman et al. (2003) wrote that it is not uncommon for an ethnographer to use several methods such as interviews, observation, participation and recording to study the same "object" in an endeavor to achieve a more thorough reflection of the complex reality: "…*each social researcher is likely to concentrate on different aspects of a 'confused reality', which is too complex to study in its entirety. A partial solution to understanding this complex reality is triangulation of methodology, which means using several methods to study the same object. If only one method would be used, the result is a 'one dimensional snapshot of a very wide and deep social scene'... "*

Shipman (1998), Atkinson (1990), Ellen (1984), Fetterman (1998), Grills (1998), Hammersley and Atkinson (1983), Thomas (1993) provide guidelines for this construction of complex reality from a social scene such as the Kenya health sector. The most striking aspect in this study (from among the many guidelines) is the note taking feature (as a generalization of the sustained writing up that was characteristic to my engagements). This is seen in my research diary, calendar entries, writing of briefs from meetings, from interviews, written summaries of telephone conversations, transcribing highlights from audio recording, research status reports, etc. These have been of great input to my reflections revealing instances that initially were surprising but over time have become usual observations.

Moreover, taking time to write down observations and reviews of achievements was a strategy that facilitated reflections that led to identification and development of ideas. Reflection supported by use of triangulation strategies in ethnography lead to unfolding what was presented by the actors by seeing beyond what is said and subjecting it to the specific interpretation that holds in the context (this would change in another context). References to earlier noted observations were great aids to this unfolding. An example is the observation of silence on the part of most participants in workshops and meetings. It was only through reflection guided by earlier taken notes in individual meetings with these participants that it became clear I was dealing with a situation of power sensitive encounters with the problem that I was "*calling upon participants to speak and not to just write down what to do next*" (Kiura 2006). This was a different experience from what they were used to in their context. This is an example of how my approach of mixed methods helped "gain a holistic perspective, through which isolated observations can only be understood in relation to other aspects of the situation" (Agar 1980), and my use of mixed methods supported that.

2.3.5. Intervention in reality

My practice and approach does not end at ethnography and associated concepts of mixed methods. Beyond just understanding the context, I was engaged in activities that were changing it. Kensing et al. (1996) argue that "... *ethnography and Intervention contrast in terms of their basic approaches and intended results: ethnographers originally strove not to change the phenomena they were studying, while interventionists deliberately set up activities to change the organization in order to learn from the reactions to the change".*

Whereas the results of ethnographic studies can be termed as descriptive from details collected by researchers while immersed in the studied contexts, the constructive nature of my work only uses these results as ground work for engaging in a change-oriented approach that look beyond the accounts of the status quo in the context. The holistic descriptions of the accounts required subjection of other practices that drew inspirations from research strategies orientated towards generation of theory. Moreover, from the initial experiences at the hospital, the knowledge from the sector informed the approaches in other projects and subsequent reflection to build new understanding of project establishment. I describe this as an application of the single-loop and double-loop learning concepts.

2.3.6. Grounded theory

The theoretical results of this study, having been developed on empirical data and experiences, can be said to be inspired by the principles of grounded theory (Glaser & Strauss 1967). The general understanding of grounded theory is that it involves the collection of small amount of data and the subsequent exploration of underlying concepts. Using grounded theory strategy means that theories are derived from the data and later applied to larger sets of data (Orlikowski 1993).

As described in the first project, a lot of empirical data was collected and experiences therein are the basis of the insights that inform the practice of the other projects in the sector. These informed practices and reported results in this study resonate with Thoresen (1999)'s definition of grounded theory as an approach for generating theory from collected situational data, *"discovered, developed and provisionally verified through systematic data collection and analysis of data pertaining to that phenomenon. . . . One does not begin with a theory and then prove it. Rather, one begins with an area of study and what is relevant to that area is allowed to emerge"* (as cited in Cockburn 2003, p.).

The theoretical sensitivity necessary in grounded theory was acquired via in-depth study of participatory design methods, especially the Scandinavian approach and the STEPS methodology; knowledge management and knowledge representation; Joint Applications Design (Wood and Silver 1995); approaches to development in developing countries (Dahms and Faust-Ramos 2002, Sen 2000) among others. Moreover, technically I was supported by a solid background in software engineering with practical experiences in such software development approaches as framework-based development of (web) applications. **Figure** 4 below summarizes a schematic view of my research practice.

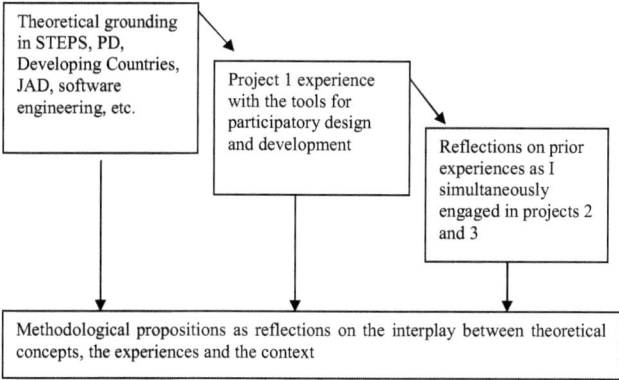

Figure 4: **Schematic representation of my research practice**

The initial assumptions on the research approach were strongly challenged by the actual experiences in the context with the consequence that this influenced the lessons that can be drawn from the study, cf. (Thoresen 1999) "... *research cannot always choose its approach and topics independently when the project has an action interest. Research must, to some extent, adapt to the knowledge requirements that are imposed by the action aspect.*"

The process to these redirections and developments has a lot of similarities to the concepts of single-loop and double-loop learning for unfolding reality in context-specific situations that demand interventions and concrete methodologies for informing practice. Next I present my application of these concepts.

2.4. Research activity as learning, adapting and changing the rules

2.4.1. From using STEPS to doing 'JAD STEPS'

Single-loop learning means that in the event of a problem, a solution can be found there and then. In this form of learning, people (actors) are primarily considering their actions. Small changes are made to specific practices or behaviors, based on what has or has not worked in the past. This involves doing things better without necessarily examining or challenging the underlying beliefs and assumptions. The goal is improvements that often take the form of procedures or rules (Argyris et al. 1985). In my study, an example of this was found in the many instances that I had to adapt my speed, my expectations and presentation methods in interacting with project stakeholders. In most cases, these adaptations were aimed at accomplishing the tasks at hand – such as concluding a workshop or interview on a positive note.

I achieved this without any critical reflections on developments behind the interview or workshop. Model developments, necessitating adjustments included felt antagonism from participants; silence when i asked questions; last minute changes to meetings agendas featuring both additions of demands and reductions of outputs (deliverables). A noticeable sample adjustment on the methodological approach (tool) is my choice to engage a combination of STEPS and JAD in my approaches. This was partly motivated by the fact that JAD was specific in proposing concrete steps that came in handy in 'surprise' moments.

An example of surprise moment is the need to describe workshop (design) process and not to just perform the workshop (design) sessions. This required that I take as point of departure, what was familiar to the participants. This reflection is generally similar to what Schön (1983, p.26) describes as reflection in action. *"... that process that allows us to reshape what we are working on, while we are working on it. It is that on-going experimentation that helps us find a viable solution. In this, we do not use a "trial-and-error" method. Rather, our actions are much more reasoned and purposeful than that. If something isn't working correctly (doesn't seem right, doesn't seem to move you closer to the goal) then you "reflect" (a conscious activity) in the action-present".*

After such instances, I was engaged in processes of reflection that questioned whether I was doing things the right way. This questioning was followed by engaging changes in my adopted ways. This is what is referred to as double-loop learning in the literature. *"In double-loop learning, members of the organization are able to reflect on whether the 'rules' themselves should be changed, not only on whether deviations have occurred and how to correct them. This kind of learning involves more 'thinking outside the box,' creativity and critical thinking. This learning often helps participants understand why a particular solution works better than others to solve a problem or achieve a goal"* (Schön 1983, p. 26).

In my case, it meant that I had to engage JAD in STEPS and also deal with the question of whether I was focusing on the underlying factors leading to the negative experiences with the partners in such workshop settings. It involved repeated discussions (in cycles) that resulted to a major change in my engagements. I had to review the project timelines, and my adoption of their 'known' communication approaches and pace of working. These were eye-opening reflections for me as they brought to fore the intricate issues that needed to be addressed in the context pointing to the best ways to engage interactions with people whose daily work lives are embedded around those issues.

With such soul-searching questions as: What is happening? What are the patterns from my encounters? What can I learn from the patterns? I was able to identify three underlying issues that were besetting my work. These are described in (Kiura 2006) and are: the issue of power index dimensions in understanding national cultures (Hofstede 1991); the issue of democracy and empowerment at the work place as an indispensable and a preamble requirement for embracing participation in information systems design in the sector (Bjerknes and Bratteteig 1995) and the third issue was the realization that I had to embrace an incremental system development concept that is based on viewing the information system as a whole of various semi-autonomous component parts that should be developed in a sequence of increments in a way that supports learning in making the transitions (Krabbel, Wetzel & Ratuski 1997).

2.4.2. Research approach overview

In summary, for data collection I followed the principles and methods drawn from: action research, ethnography, case study and grounded theory. In order to understand the empirical experiences, the concepts that come to play include: single and double-loop learning; reflection-on-action and reflection-on-action. Reflection-in-action as experienced in the hospital

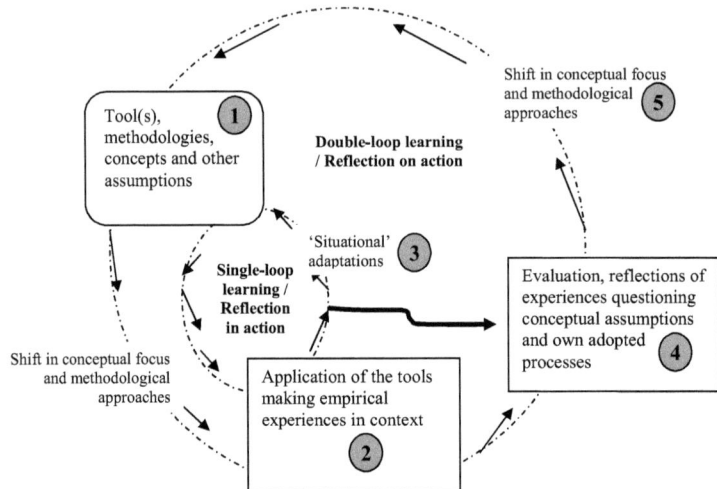

information system project and reflection-on-action as espoused by the application of insights from the previous projects in the consequent projects.

Figure 5: Summary of research practice overview

Figure 5 presents a condensed overview of my research practice. I started with a set of assumptions that are represented by my theoretical grounds in STEPS, participatory design, development approaches, developing countries, JAD, software engineering and other assumptions not only those specific to this study but also those drawn from other skills and previous experiences . Once in the research context, my activities were a reflection of this initial set of knowledge (assumptions) being applied in the reality of the context. In the engagements, situations of "surprise" arose that called for immediate adaptations to 'survive situations'. These I understand as processes of single-loop learning or reflections-in-action. In **Figure 5** this is depicted by the inner circle. As I continued with the empirical experiences, I did not remain in the inner circle but the context called for me to evaluate, reflect and question not only the assumptions I brought to the study, but also the processes (and strategies) of engagement that I was adapting.

The result of this was a shift of my underlying conceptual assumptions and methodological approaches that I understand as processes of double-loop learning (the outer larger circle). My approach can be seen to fit the approach of collaborative research practice (Mathiassen 2000), which is an application of the principles of reflective systems development (RSD) method (Mathiassen 1998) drawn from Schön's (1983, 1987) notion of the reflective practitioner.

2.5. Discussion and chapter closing

From the study design and the selection of the cases used as empirical material, the experiences reported in the project establishment exercises build on each other. Subsequent experiences build on insights from the earlier ones. The issues that confronted my practice, spanning from technical and social cultural aspects of project practice in developing countries, made my research experiences complex. My drawing of inspiration from grounded theory is to be understood as an attempt to seek an inductive approach that could generate patterns and hypotheses from my qualitative findings that centered on the organizational (sector) context.

The research's initial objective to identify enrichments to the STEPS methodology was being shifted to take a process view (Markus & Robey 1988) that was opening up the methodology to the extent that the empirical experiences demanded concrete propositions of practicing the methodology. These, to the best of my knowledge are implied in the methodological definition of STEPS. The process view shift called for understanding the choices that have to be made in specific situations of using the methodology to achieve conception, design and deployment of IT interventions. This shift was especially necessary as the contextual issues overturned previous assumptions on participation. The assumptions were challenged when applied as a means to adapt to such power intensive contexts coupled with the identified complexity of communication and information sharing, design of work and work processes in the prevailing relationships that the participants find themselves in.

The process view exposed the need to understand the attitudes as they unfolded and shifted over time enabling predictions on similar situations in the same sector and the country in general. Whereas the adopted research practice and approach might be considered weak in making a strong case for generalizing the results, my response is that the value of my results is to be found not in their complete generality, but in the contextual insights they expose and the propositions that I describe. The lessons learnt from this study are intended to be convincing contributions to ongoing discussions in the technological, organizational, and policy fields in establishing projects. I argue that for this sort of learning, the qualitative, interpretive approach that I followed here works well.

Chapter closing

In retrospect of my practice and the applied methods, I conclude that I have survived the study this far largely because these methods sought to tame the conditions of the context and to change the attitudes of the people (including me). At no time in this study is it advocated to engage in dismantling power balances. On the contrary, I argue on propositions that seek coexistence of project establishment experiences in the structures of power.

Projects have short periods to ambitiously dismantle stable and static organizational structures defined over long periods of time. The necessary changes in the structures will with time come about, emanating from the structures as they adapt themselves in much the same way as the general rule of the *"survival of the fittest"* as understood in the evolution theory.

3. Contextualized Information Systems Development

Overview
In this chapter, I make a case for contextualized information systems development. I situate this closely to research on information system development in developing countries' projects. Based on my research's grounding in the ideals of participatory design, I argue that socio-technical approaches provide a basis for a methodological focus that deals with the elusive information system development practice in contexts similar to my research context. Specifically, I situate power as a problem in socio-technical approaches emanating from organizational structure and culture. I further relate strict power relations to the realities of organizational structure and organizational culture as the basis of problems encountered in the endeavors to initiate participative practice in the Kenyan health sector. From this discussion I conclude that from a perspective of methodological approaches to initiate information system development projects in similar contexts, community based participatory design (CBPD) and STEPS provides the basic ideals that when incorporated in PD practice can mitigate issues of power. Background to this is picking of empowerment and learning as important elements for information system development methodical approaches. CBPD promotes generation of local knowledge and co-learning in projects while STEPS emphasizes communication, alignment to use context and organizational embedding in workplace arrangements.

3.1. Context issues in information systems development
In developing countries, information system development projects are a major way in which diffusion of Information Technology (IT) takes place. In the framework of a software development project, a process is undertaken through which an IT artifact is defined, developed and deployed in a given context (Mursu et al. 2000). Viewed as an instance of technology diffusion, an information system development project is more than a programming or software engineering exercise as it involves a collection of concepts, beliefs, values and principles. These are implicitly or explicitly represented in the methodological approaches used to inform the process. The results from the process are more than just a computer artifact given the effects that are instituted in an organization as the artifact interacts with people, rules, norms and commands. Mathiassen (1997) characterizes an information system development exercise as an intentional

change process based on some clear objectives meant to effect defined changes in organizations. Effects on an organization are not limited to the produced artifact but also come from the project process adopted. In this regard, Lyytinen (1987) has characterized the impacts of changes in an organization into three aspects: technical, informational and organizational. Technical aspects relate to the infrastructure platform, informational aspects relate to the contents handled by the system while organizational aspects focus on the intricacies at play as the information system gets to be used. These aspects are at play during an information system development process such that methodological approaches in the process can be understood as tools that in one way or another relate to addressing these aspects. Due to the relationship between methods and aspects prevalent in a given organizational context, methods for technology diffusion or transfer (Avgerou 1996) face the question of suitability in different contexts. By practicing information system development in a given setting, the interplay of the context features in light of the above aspects makes an information system development activity a unique undertaking. The uniqueness of the exercise means information system development methodologies are not universal but need to be adjusted to different economic, cultural and organizational settings (Avgerou 1996, Mursu et al. 2000). The uniqueness of the process in different contexts introduces special requirements on information system development methods. Special requirements mean methodological adaptations, such as identifying a suitable focus for a method to address issues prevalent in a context. This aspect of finding a methodological fit applies in a special way during project establishment as a time during which the construction of a context's reality takes place, bringing to fore salient issues that uniquely identifies the context.

To define a context in my study, I limit myself to observable organizational aspects that can be identified as special features of a given context. This research has been done in a developing country where development of information systems *"... has been difficult to achieve, and is likely to remain elusive ..."* (Braa et al. 2007 p. 381). As a technology diffusion exercise it involves actors with different perceptions of how technology is to extend their interests (Timmons 2003). The specific context in this study is the Kenyan health sector that exhibits issues of organizational structure, complexity and fuzziness as a result of cultural, social, political and moral aspects (Avison et al. 1999). Based on this, this study takes the view that suitability of methods is to be assessed on how far they enable understanding the context phenomenon by facilitating interpretation of the prevalent features. Methods for information system development practice in a context are applicable in so far as they relate to and focus on context features. Waema (1996) has argued that the differences in information systems development and use between developed and developing countries are not based on the technology itself or on proposed methods but are mainly caused by the social preconditions which challenge information system development methods and practices. In recognition that the success of a technology depends on the social structure in which it is embedded (Reddy et al. 2003) implementing a successful technology therefore requires a thorough understanding of the organizational context, such as the organization's structure, work, and employees. This understanding is therefore the basis of the special consideration that needs to be adopted in a development methodology. This calls for adaptation of the methods to take into account infrastructural, organizational, social and political differences between developed and developing countries' contexts. These differences are addressed in approaches that recognize the existence of technical and social subsystems in organizations, the so called socio-technical approaches (Avgerou et al. 2004, Cherns 1976, Clegg 2000). These approaches recognize the importance of incorporating insights from the social sciences, thus promoting a focus on the interrelation between technology and its social environment (Kaplan 1997, Lorenzi 1997).

3.2. Socio-technical approaches during project establishment

Information system development is a complex and costly endeavor. From a software engineering perspective the primary concern is to organize the software development process to maximize its efficiency and probability of success (Sommerville 2001). In the context of an information system development project, a major initial step is project establishment that is concerned with an analysis of prevailing conditions and their influence on the project execution. This involves clarifying the big picture of the project and setting up a project team (Andersen et al. 1990). A project establishment exercise in a context such as a developing country is done within contextual realities that present challenges on the application domain, the project process and associated approaches. Project establishment should take the perspective that real world settings are dynamic and unique to contexts. This close relation to context is recognized in software engineering. From Sommerville's description of requirements that should be *"... derived from the way in which people actually work rather than the way in which process definitions say they ought to work ...*" (Sommerville 2001, p. 136) it is clear that successful software engineering practice needs to promote cooperation and awareness of activities at a given context.

Heeks (2002) uses the notion of design-reality gap to explain the high rates of information system development projects failure in developing countries. Heeks concludes that a successful developing country information system is one that does not suffer from mismatch between IS designs and local user reality but one that matches its environment with regard to technical, social and organizational factors such as the values, perceptions and assumptions of the project stakeholders. Endeavors to achieve this match are to be found in socio-technical approaches that recognize the existence and interdependence of technical and social subsystems in organizations (Clegg 2000). During project establishment, the problem of the mismatch can be addressed by exposing organizational realities. Specifically this study proposes as a way to this, the opening of communication channels to and between project stakeholders who are closest to the context of implementation and use. The intention is to not only describe an organizational reality, but to understand the multiple organizational realities of those involved in the project. This has consequences to the relations between the project stakeholders thereby encouraging them to articulate the difference between rational and prescriptive models of what they should be doing and real depictions of what they actually do.

Developing countries cannot be rightly characterized as representing a homogenous context. The realities differ from region to region and even within a given region different sectors are likely to have differences of prevalent cultures. In this regard, my experiences are explicitly in the health sector. Problems in information technology usage in Health care sector have been identified to include: fragmented industry structure, big national differences in processes, strong professional culture of medical care personnel, one-sided education, handcrafting traditions, weak customers, and hierarchical organization structures (Suomi 2000). This list presents issues that range from micro to macro issues all with a strong influence on the success or failure of an information system development project (Balka 2003). Moreover, such aspects as the financial status of a health organization and the personality of a project leader are related to wider issues of national and organizational culture respectively (Balka 2003, Ellingsen & Monteiro 2003). Through socio-technical approaches, PD ideals are promoted as users take the lead in IS design with the objective to ensure that the tools developed support their needs and interests that they represent in their work environments (Greenbaum & Kyng 1996, Asaro 2000).

Much of the research in health institutions related to power issues has addressed problems of professional cultures, recognizing strong professional cultures in health care settings especially between doctors and nurses (Martin and Siehl 1983). Strong hierarchical, professional, and specialized sector structures are all part of broader social and cultural issues that complicate IS development and application. These can be summarized as bureaucratic problems that affect ways of working and consequently the design and development of information systems (Middleton 1999). This study takes a structuration (Giddens 1986, Orlikowski 2000) view of the power problem in the health sector based on the argument that given the way the health sector is structured, health facilities are seldom able to carry out the work of system development in isolation. They must interact with (and sometimes comply with) other institutions and structures including national regulations and other decision making bodies in the hierarchy. The structures and institutions might play a facilitative role during an information system's development project or significantly change the environment in which system is not only developed but also deployed (Balka 2003). Such hierarchically structured organizations with strict communication channels through which information is expected to flow present special cases of information systems project processes. This is partly through the development of an information system, changes are effected in organizations (Orlikowski et al. 1995) making it a political process. Relationships, patterns of communication, of influence, authority, and control are altered through information systems. Implementation strategies must therefore deal with politics of conflicting priorities, objectives, and values prevalent in organizations where the project is taking place (Keen 1981). Whereas the politics involved in information system development projects could be traced to various organizational realities, this study deals with these politics from a power perspective as influenced by the organizational structure in place.

3.3. Power issues from organizational structure and culture

The relationship of organizational structures in defining power issues in organizations can be traced back to "Leavitt's Diamond" that structures an organization into four closely related components of Tasks, Structure, Technology and People **(Figure 6)**. According to this representation, when a change takes place in any of the four corners of this diamond, the other components adjust in response (Leavitt 1965 as used in Keen 1981).

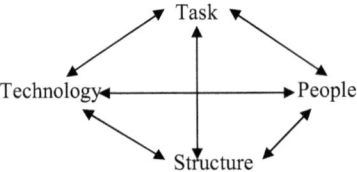

Figure 6: Leavitt "Diamond": Components of the organization (Keen 1981 p. 25)

From this relation, information technology implementation influences the organizational structures in place just as other components are affected when an organization embraces use of technology. Generally technology systems necessitate changes in organizations; changes that must be negotiated as they intrude into the hitherto realities of organizational structures (Keen 1981). Any such effects on the equilibrium status of organization structures lead to confrontation with power relations prevalent in organization structures.

Organizational structures institutionalize how people interact with each other, how communication flows and how power relationships are defined (Hall 1987 as used in Zhang et al. 2004). Based on this, organizational structures can be classified depending on the nature of interactions and relations they impart on their employees. According to Khandwalla (1977)'s classification, organizational structures can take many forms, ranging from highly mechanistic to highly organic. Mechanistic structures are typically highly formalized, non-participative, hierarchical, tightly controlled, and inflexible. Organic structures, on the other hand, are characterized by informality, decentralization of authority, open channels of communication, and flexibility. Participation and group consensus is favored by organic structures that are open and have free flow of information throughout the organization with operational details being largely decided upon at operational levels. The health sector that forms the empirical background for this study can be considered to have characteristics of mechanistic structure. One strong reality at the health sector is that of strict power relations. These are understood from the perspective of how the sector is structured and consequently the channels of communication and information flow. In such a scenario, contradictory interests or at least contradictory perceptions of interests confront information system development projects' establishment. In the rush to initiate a project whereby sometimes budgetary issues or other pressures come up, the interests and powers of different participating stakeholders can be easily overlooked. The danger is that manifestations of power in these groups will be taken for granted, misunderstood or ignored which may lead to failure, troubled relations during the project among other undesirable effects. I present my understanding of the realities of power in the operations of the sector summarized into perspectives of **contending, yielding and avoiding**. Contending is represented by one party imposing its preferred perspectives in the process. Yielding is exhibited by some parties (stakeholders) adjusting to the demands of the other party by submitting to the will of those with power. Avoiding is represented by withdrawal from conflicts and change of focus on how an issue is addressed. Such an issue remains upheld at the background since it can't be accommodated by the normal and accepted relations in the sector. To address these perspectives, engagements that work over time to accommodate shifting perceptions through dialogue are proposed to ensure successful initiation of projects. This proposition follows the adjustment of methodological approaches focus to bring out issues underlying yielding, contending and avoiding when an IS design expert is engaged in processes to initiate a project.

3.3.1. Organizational culture

Related to how people behave in the course of their work in organizations is the notion of culture as an underlying determinant of how persons perceive their environments. Culture can be broadly understood as *"a set of basic tacit assumptions about how the world is and ought to be that a group of people share and that determines their perceptions, thoughts, feelings, and, to some degree, their overt behavior"* (Schein 1996 in Keyton 2005). According to Hofstede (1991) there are three main factors that, at least to some degree, determine the behavior of a person in the workplace: national culture, occupational culture, and organizational culture. National culture is based primarily on differences in values which are learned in early childhood from the family. These values are strong enduring beliefs which are unlikely to change throughout the person's life. Occupational culture, which is acquired through schooling and professional training between childhood and adulthood, is comprised of both values and shared practices. Shared practices are learned perceptions as to how things should be done in the context of some occupation and are as such malleable from training. Organizational culture is based on differences in norms and shared practices which are learned in the workplace and are considered as valid within the boundaries of a particular organization (Mintzberg 1978, Schein 1996, Trice & Beyer 1993).

From the point of view of technology design and implementation, national culture can be an important issue in transferring technology across nations, designing systems with culturally diverse teams or deploying systems for users from different cultural environments. This study therefore takes a special consideration of organizational culture in studying a methodological approach outside its development context. Organizational culture comprises of a set of social norms that implicitly define what behaviors are appropriate or inappropriate within the boundaries of the organization. From my experiences I am framing this organizational culture to the organizational structure in place.

One of the key determinants of organizational culture is the way in which the organization manages its employees, in other words, the organization's structure of its workforce. The structure to a large extent influences the management and operational processes in an organization. Through this, the organization sends messages to the employees as to what behaviors are considered desirable and, hence, they determine the shared practices which define, according to Hofstede (1991), the organization's culture. By the time a person enters the organization, their national and professional cultures are already in place whereas organizational culture can be at modified. This potential manageability of organizational culture makes it particularly interesting from the point of view of implementing technology-driven change and for this study as a basis to inform information system development methods to suit cultures in different contexts. Aligning a methodology of practice and organizational culture is not an easy task, partly because they both interact with other key organizational subsystems to the extent of sometimes being seen to challenge the formal structure, procedures, processes and the strategic intent of the organization. Therefore, this study concentrates on being aware of these other organizational subsystems but specializes at this point to concern itself with the general organizational culture.

Why is organizational culture so important from the point of view of establishing information system development projects? A new project setting can impact the very nature of relations in an organization to the extent that new relationships amongst the stakeholders are expected. Whether or not an information system development project takes off and the stakeholders collaborate for results will in part depend on whether the cultural changes it imposes (by challenging the status quo) can be accommodated in the project team. This challenge is manifested in changes that introduction of a technology brings about in organizations. Cabrera et al. (2001) argue that the changes to organizations as a result of technology can be mediated by seeking to achieve **vertical** and **horizontal** fits. By Vertical fit means that the changes must seek to align to the organization's strategy, capabilities and infrastructure. Horizontal fit on the other hand is achieved through alignment to the social and technical components of the organization. This study makes contributions to how methodological approaches can be enriched to facilitate achievement of not only the horizontal fit but also the vertical fit. The contribution is framed in the recognition of the organization structure's influence to the prevalent culture that consequently determines how project stakeholders relate and interact in a project.

3.3.2. Power distance index dimension of culture

Whereas I give organization culture a special recognition here, it is important to note that the cultural effects identified as influencing project establishment in my study are not exclusively attributed to organizational culture. National culture prevalent in the Kenya health sector also contributes to explain the realities of strict power relations. A much cited study on national cultures is that by Hofstede (1980). From a collection of over 100,000 questionnaires from over 60 countries Hofstede identified four basic areas that present dimensions of culture in organizations. These dimensions present aspects of culture that can be measured relative to other cultures. These four dimensions are (Hofstede 1980 p.85):-

- Power distance index – the degree of inequality of power between a person at a higher level and a person at a lower level
- Individualism – the relative importance of individual goals compared with group or collective goals
- Masculinity – the extent to which the goals of men dominate those of women
- Uncertainty avoidance - the extent to which future possibilities are defended against or accepted

From statistical analysis, different countries were identified to have different scores for the above dimensions and therefore depicting differences in their national cultures. From a perspective of strict power relations in the Kenyan health sector I pick on Hofstede's power distance index dimension and highlight a comparison of selected countries and regions **(Table 1)**.

Country/Region	Power Distance Index	Country/Region	Power Distance Index
Malaysia	104	Thailand	64
Guatemala	95	South Africa	49
United Arab Emirates		USA	40
Ecuador	78	Canada	39
India	77	(West) Germany	35
West Africa	77	Great Britain	35
France	68	Finland	33
Colombia	67	Norway	31
East Africa	64	Denmark	18
Peru	64	Austria	11

Table 1: Power distance index of selected countries (adapted from Hofstede, 1991 p. 85)

Power distance index can be understood as "the extent to which less powerful members of institutions and organizations within a country expect and accept that power is distributed unequally" (Hofstede 1991, p. 262). The index describes also the extent to which employees lower in a hierarchy accept that superiors have more power than they have and consequently opinions and decisions are right because they come from higher positions of the hierarchy. For example, from the **Table 1** it shows that in comparison, the East African region to a higher degree accepts and expects that power is distributed unequally as compared to such countries as Finland, Norway, Sweden, Germany, USA. A larger power distance index indicates that the relationships are strict; the boss is powerful and cannot be criticized. Formal relationships exist whereby the less powerful members of organizations and institutions accept and expect that power is unequally distributed. Hofstede found out that in countries with a high power distance index, organizations have highly hierarchical structures and 'followers' (those in lower levels of the hierarchy) endorse the superiors' power, authority and influence. This relates directly to our experience.

My experience in the course of this study confirms Hofstede's results on realities of power distance in the relationships amongst the players in the Kenyan health sector. In the sector, work settings stress vertical lines of communication which presents problems in adopting PD practices that assume everyone has access to and talks with everyone during projects (Adler 1986). In such situations, the very core understanding of an information systems' contribution in the operations of the organization is that it will help information be available to management (higher levels). By being aware of the power distance index and how power relations are defined, an information system designer is able to foresee some of the dangers inherent in a context and adapt methodologies accordingly.

In the background of strict power relations and vertical lines of communication prevalent in the Kenyan health sector, initiating interactions, building and maintaining project group cohesion are not trivial tasks. Successful project establishment therefore seeks to elicit adequate levels of motivation on the part of the full range of those involved in the project, irrespective of positions in the hierarchy. Colucci (2003) has described the importance of nurturing motivation as willingness of organizational members to exercise their skills and energies in reference to the stated objectives of a particular project. This relates to questions of ownership and identification with the project. Colucci (2003) describes two sorts of motivation: compliance and commitment. Compliance is described as behavior in response to authoritative directives and regulated by the terms of the employment contract. It is associated with how the organization functions within established relationships. Commitment, on the other hand, is associated with organizational innovation and change in relationships. In power intensive contexts compliance to established rules and procedures is the norm, initial endeavors to initiate a project in the sector were limited to such realities as described in project 1. Participatory design approaches in such contexts needs to be suited to handle and respond in reaction to relational dispositions of the actors especially as they remain embedded in organizational social processes in the course of the project. This means structural realities of hierarchical command-control; authoritative structures are important parameters influencing the success of the approaches adopted for mobilizing and sustaining support for project establishment. Such structures create social distance that undermines social interaction processes and hence participation in project groups.

Structurally defined power relations introduce problems of social distance between project stakeholders when they carry hierarchical realities of relations to a project. In recognition of these problems (Bjerknes & Bratteteig 1995) here argued that democracy and empowerment at the work place are indispensable as a preamble for embracing participation in information systems design and development. Once one starts to bring together a group of project stakeholders into a forum where expression is supposed to be a norm, a political dimension sets in, characterized by efforts towards more democratic space at work. This is especially the case in my case study settings with a high power distance index (see East Africa in **Table 1**). When future system users are invited to influence a system's design and development, it necessarily means that they are being invited to wield and exercise power to make decisions touching on appraisal of their work settings, their work organization, and the priority areas of the system under design. This causes tension with the status quo of the organization as described in (Kiura 2006). To promote foundational elements of a democratic society during information system development projects, inclusive approaches are necessary.

Faced with these challenges of lacking democratic space at work and interaction inhibiting power relations that do not promote practice of PD, I find evolutionary methods as being suited in the contexts. As foundational elements for methods suitable for such contexts, I pick out empowerment and learning. These two elements are important as background ideals of methodological approaches used to set pace in promotion of participation by expanding democratic space in the context. These should be adopted as central elements for informing a context sensitive and development-from-within methodological approach for project establishment (Dahms & Faust-Ramos 2002). By evolutionary approaches I refer to approaches that are *"more flexible rather than predictive, they emphasize participative communication and learning process, use context (workplace and application orientation), visioning and organizational embedding"* (Biru 2008, p. 7). As examples from the PD community I especially find this to resonate with the Software Technology for Evolutionary Participative System Development (STEPS) proposed by Floyd et al. (1989a), and Reflective System Development (Mathiassen 1998). These methods, especially STEPS promote incorporation of learning in information system development and hence facilitate technology diffusion during projects.

The thrust of the two elements of empowerment and learning that I stress here is to be understood as representing a paradigmatic focus that closely encompasses knowledge generation in social actions (praxis) whereby project contexts are at the forefront of knowledge generation and validation. This line of argumentation can be found in Dewey (1991) and Greenwood & Levin (1998) who argue that democratization can be achieved through new knowledge generation in social action. It is through the promotion of participation with project stakeholders in project planning that we can have a practice that has a genuine context-sensitive focus. This is achievable though a methodology that empowers the stakeholders. It is upon these two elements of empowerment and learning that I refer to the ideals of community based participatory design (CBPD) to derive inspirations that I propose as forming a basis for successful project establishment.

3.4. Evolutionary approaches for empowerment and learning: CBPD and STEPS

Originating from working with oppressed people in developing countries (Fals-Borda 2001) community-based participatory research (CBPR) incorporates ideals that resonate strongly with the issues in the (case study) context of this study. Ideals of participative education and social action when integrated in systems development will go a long way in mitigating issues that PD practice in developing countries face. I understand CBPD as an orientation that promotes relationships between project partners with principles of co-learning, pursuance of a common and mutual benefit founded on a long-term commitment that incorporates local expertise into project processes (Israel et al. 2003). Coming predominantly from the work of Freire (1970) on critical pedagogy that promotes dialogue, praxis, experience and promotion of generation of community based knowledge, CBPD is appealing to inform information system development practices in developing countries in general and the Kenyan health sector in particular. Freire's seminal work, *Pedagogy of the Oppressed*, is rich in inspiration for projects working with people who do not have a voice, which is a characteristic of situations of strict power relations especially at lower levels. *Pedagogy of the Oppressed* promotes the primacy of the experience of participants (originally in an educational process) as a tool to empower them (Ataöv & Haider 2006). Through collective self inquiry and reflection, project stakeholders embrace co-learning in their interactions as a project consciously relates to the context realities through actual lived experiences, opening up avenues to collaborate and participate irrespective of power relations.

This self-inquiry and reflection in continuous cycles of action and reflection by participants can mitigate project encounters for usefulness, validity and alignment to social realities of an organization context e.g. as proposed in Reflective Steps by Biru (2008).

Learning is an important aspect in the contextual realities experienced in the Kenyan health sector by promoting genuine partnership. Moreover, embrace of co-learning ensures capacity building not only for stakeholders with respect to new technologies but also for technology information systems experts with regard to competency in the organizational realities of projects. Given the political dimension of technology introduction, the project process right from initiation should seek promotion of negotiation to balance benefits and fulfillment of diverse interests from the project stakeholders. This orientation as a paradigm is a broad and adaptive methodical approach as proposed in STEPS to include among others: participative communication learning processes, orientation to workplaces with a vision for close organizational embedding (Floyd 1989a). When such are incorporated and pursued consistently and systematically at project establishment stage, the benefits of projects can be derived by stakeholders in shorter time cycles, even if the full project objective is a long-term process. Self-reflection and mutual dialogue, will offer project participants opportunities to challenge differences of domain-specific expertise, and identities in prevalent organizational power structures. Consequently this will expose complexities of project settings as a first step to mitigate underlying issues. To realize these objectives of firm embedding in organizational contexts it's important that a project establishment exercise thoroughly understands, presents and communicates the organizational realities.

Conclusion

In this chapter, an attempt was made to define context issues in information systems development. It has detailed the organizational context found in developed and developing counties by giving credence to socio-technical approaches that take into account infrastructural, organizational, social and political differences. We have seen how power relations create social distance between project stakeholders and this ideally affects information system development. In the next chapter, I present experiences of analyzing the Kenyan health sector as my context. I present the sector's stakeholders, structures and networks and how I understand their interactions in the course of projects reported in this study.

4. The Kenya Health Sector: Structure, Actor Networks, and Interaction-Moments during Project Establishment

This study is concerned with how the relationships amongst the stakeholders in the health sector affect their ability to participate effectively. The point of departure is that participatory design actors are defined by their contexts, their interests, values and rules of engagement that are best understood by prevailing interaction conditions. I draw on the sector's organization structure and then represent the relations prevalent in the project settings. I have found out that this prevalent organization structure is one manifestation of power sensitivity that is seen in the sector networks and affects interrelation of project stakeholders. In participatory design based on project establishment, the motivation is to cultivate participation that adds value to the project's administrative processes and achievement of project goals.

In this section, I describe in detail the Kenya Health sector with emphasis on the prevailing networks amongst the stakeholders. I identify strict power relations as one major feature in the sector and generally in developing countries' public healthcare institutions. In the study of Smith (1997) it was found that strict power relations are a prevalent characteristic in developing countries' health sectors. The relationships which the sector's stakeholders find themselves in, influence their ability to conceive personal and organizational development in the course of their work. The analysis will be based on two theoretical frameworks: the Mikropolis Model (Krause et al. 2006) and the Actor Network Theory (Callon 1986a). The Mikropolis Model will be used as a lens to bring out the static nature of the network in the sector. ANT will be used to analyze the network features and consequently bring out power relations in the project contexts. We shall employ the Actor Network Theory (ANT) to analyze the power relations in the context of three case study projects. The nature of interactions that people develop while working is one sure differentiating characteristic in organizations.

In the later part of the chapter, I argue that projects are defined in terms of interaction-moments exhibited in the networks that form during project establishment. I identify three interaction-moments. Their identification and the understanding of the specific features of each moment provide strategies to defuse power issues in projects spanning several organizations (or generally sector-wide projects). Strategies targeted at specific moments will operate at a level above preoccupation with power structures and chains of command in the sector.

4.1. The Kenyan Health Sector

4.1.1. Broad sector players

The World Health Organization (WHO) defines a health system as *all the activities whose primary purpose is to promote, restore or maintain health* (WHO 2000). The health sector is therefore comprised of all the groups and institutions that provide healthcare services, regulate and finance health actions right from the household to the national levels. It also includes all the activities whose primary purpose is to promote, maintain, and restore health, responsiveness, and fairness in health resources distribution. Based on this broad definition from the WHO, the Kenya health care system can be divided into three distinct groups, namely: the government (representing the public health service structures), the private organizations (both for profit and not-for profit organizations) and the donors (see **Figure 7**). The government grouping is by large represented by the Ministry of Health (MoH). There are however other governmental health service providers such as the ministry of local government, health schemes at other ministries and parastaltals that fall under those ministries. The private sector includes the medical services provided directly by private health facilities and health professionals in private practices. These are also referred to as the private-for-profit-sector health services providers. There is an unofficial sub sector comprising of institutions and providers of traditional medicine consisting of herbalists, spiritual healers and other practitioners. These are left out in the analysis of this study. Their regulation is embedded in the ministry of culture and social services. The donors comprise organizations providing international support to the sector. These are commonly referred to as "Health Development Partners". They include bilateral government to government donor agents and multilateral donor agents.

Kenya Health Sector Stakeholders	
Public Health Services **Ministry of Health (MoH)**	**Donors** **Health Development partners**
- Central MoH: the nerve center of the public health services in the country. Functional departments include: preventative and promotive health services, curative and rehabilitative services, research, standards and regulatory services, administration, etc - Parastatals – these are company like agencies owned and wholly controlled by the government. They include Kenya Medical Research Institute (KEMRI), Kenya Medical Supplies Association (KEMSA), National Hospital Insurance Fund (NHIF) among others - Provincial and district organization units – these are health departments in the decentralized government structures in different geographical regions - Health facilities – these are public health services facilities that are owned and run by the government	- Bilateral donors: agents used by governments to fund or deliver their country of origin's development assistance to the Kenyan health sector - Multilateral donors: international agencies whose funding come from several foreign governments and world bodies such the United Nations and implement development assistance in the health sector.
	Private Health Service providers
	- Private for Profit: private hospitals and other facilities as well as general practitioner clinics - Private not for profit: Both local and international organizations. They include: Faith Based Organizations (FBOs), Civil Society Organizations (CSOs), community, national and international non-governemental organizations.

Figure 7: Major Kenya Health sector stakeholders

4.1.2. Public health system decision-making structures

The organizational structure of the Kenyan public health care system is hierarchical comprising various levels of administration. **Figure** 8 depicts a simplified representation of the sector's decision making structures from the top political governance and management level to the lower levels represented by health services consumers. The hierarchy is embodied in the general management and administrative decision chains with policy directions flowing from the top (ministerial level) to the bottom. In addition, the hierarchy also adheres to the service access structure whereby: health services clients access the health system by starting at the bottom and move upwards as the health need gets more complex, by a referral procedure [see **Figure 10**].

At each level of the system, decision making, management, and service delivery functions require close interactions among the key health sector and health-related stakeholders. An actor in the sector can bring about changes in the sector depending on the position in the public health sector organizational hierarchy.

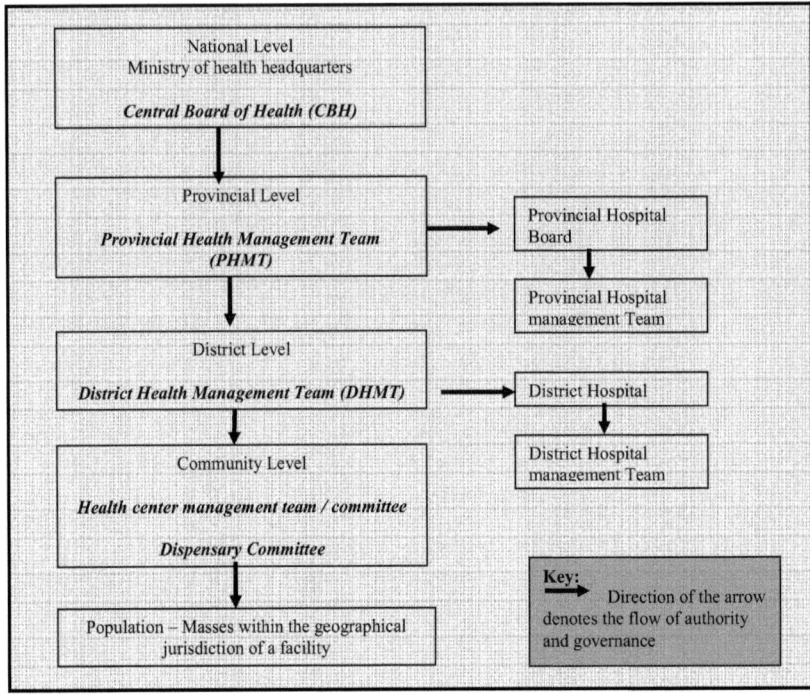

Figure 8: Structure of decision making and public health services provision in the sector

4.1.3. Sector tiers and functions

Oyaya & Rifkin (2003) have identified the four broad tiers into which the Kenya health system is organized. These are the national, provincial, district and community tiers. **Figure 9** summarizes the functional responsibilities of the various tiers in the sector. From this structure of the health system, administrative tasks are done in the national, provincial and district tiers. Direct provision of health services takes place at the facilities across the country. Consequently, I have in this text adopted the term "Facility level" to represent what Oyaya and Rifkin refers to as the "Community level".

Tier	Structure	Functions
National	Central Board of Health	Policy formulation; strategic planning; regulatory control; coordination of human resource development; resource mobilization; donor relations
Provincial	Provincial Health Management Board/ Team	Supervision and support of regional and district activities; implementation and enforcement of health standards and regulations; Inspectorate for monitoring health system performance; management and financial audit; continuing education; on job training; action research
District	District Health Management Board/Team	Administer cost sharing schemes; oversee planning, governance, management and development of health services in the district; allocation and distribution of resources; make recommendations on expenditures and budgets; implementing and monitoring all health activities in the district; reporting, generating and controlling expenditures of voted financial resources
Facility	Facility health committee. Also referred to as community or village health management committees for health centers or dispensaries	Development, governance, financing and sustaining community level health services

Figure 9: Levels of authority and decision-making (adapted from Oyaya & Rifkin 2003)

In summary, the organization of the health care delivery system revolves around three levels: the Ministry of Health (MoH) headquarters, the provinces and districts. The headquarter sets policies, coordinates all health activities in the sector including policy formulation, policies implementation, management, monitoring and evaluation. The provincial tier acts as an intermediary between the central ministry and the districts. It oversees the implementation of health policy at the regional and district level, maintains quality standards and coordinates and controls all district health activities. In addition, it monitors and supervises district health management boards (DHMBS) that in turn supervise the operation of health activities at the district level. The district level concentrates on facilitating delivery of health care services, generating their own expenditure plans and budget requirements based on the guidelines from the headquarters through the provinces. The facilities are the contact points for healthcare services by the communities in this arrangement.

4.1.4. Access to the health services

In terms of access to (and delivery of) service, the health system in Kenya is organized and implemented through a network of facilities organized in a pyramidal pattern (**Figure 10**). The service system structures are pyramidal in the sense that they are bulky at the bottom and thin out towards the top (Wamai 2004). This is a direct consequence of the above discussed hierarchical nature of the sector structure. The network starts from dispensaries and health clinics at the bottom. Dispensaries and health centers provide the bulk of health services as the first level of contact with the community. The sub-district and district hospitals form the next layer followed by the provincial hospitals. They both provide referral and outpatient services in addition to the requisite technical backstopping to dispensaries, clinics and health centers in their respective geographical areas of jurisdiction. Kenyatta national hospital and Moi teaching and referral hospital are at the apex as national referral, research and teaching facilities. Facilities become more and more sophisticated in diagnostic, therapeutic and rehabilitative services at the upper levels.

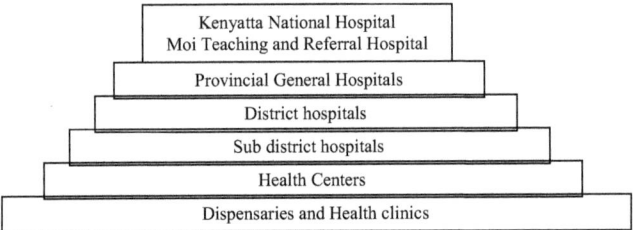

Figure 10: Network of facilities in the Kenya health sector

4.2. Mikropolis Model as an analytical tool to my work

4.2.1. The Mikropolis Model

The Mikropolis Model described here originated as a didactical instrument in higher education aimed at explaining the interplay among computing activities, human beings and the global society within the same systemic context. The model was developed by the research group headed by Prof. Dr. Arno Rolf in the University of Hamburg. It is used in the University of Hamburg as an orientation model for students of Computer Science and Business Informatics courses. It has also been published by the German Federal Agency for Civic Education (Rolf 2004). The name Mikropolis is derived from the German term "Mikroelektronik" (microelectronics) and the Greek word *polis* thus emphasizing the necessity to consider not only technical aspects of information technology systems but the interplay between social and technological implications. The model promotes sharing of a common understanding that designers and developers of software and information technology must take into account the social and organizational conditions as well as the consequences of technology use. This understanding is promoted by integrating different perspectives and theoretical approaches for describing socio-technical phenomena.

The model makes an analytical distinction between the macro- and micro-context of socio-technical interplay, referring these to societal and organizational perspectives respectively. This recognizes the wider scope of influence from information technology use beyond a single organization (or organization unit) to the wider societal influence. **Figure 11,** reproduced from (Krause et al. 2006) as published in (Porto & Simon 2007) illustrates the main elements of the model.

At the center we have the socio-technical core that represents the interplay between two systems that form the micro-context: the *application context* in specific organizations (with actual actors or stakeholders) and the technical *information technology (IT) systems context* generally understood as responsible for producing the technical artifact. The micro-context looks at how the shaping of human behavior and technological artifacts is interwoven: the interplay between technology realizations and their embedding (use) in organizational contexts. These features are embedded in the wider social context of the macro-context, represented in the figure by the viewpoint of the global society. At the societal level of analysis of computerization the focus is on the socio-political and socio-economic context in which the organizations are embedded. The Mikropolis Model recognizes social and political norms, cultural habits and values, and the economic pressures of a globalized world. The macro-context perspectives will enrich technology projects by facilitating consideration of factors and conditions that are relevant to the actors' actions in the micro-context but which originate in the wider societal or sectoral contexts. Consequently, embrace of technological transformation in single organizational units brings forth transformations and influences in the larger social sphere.

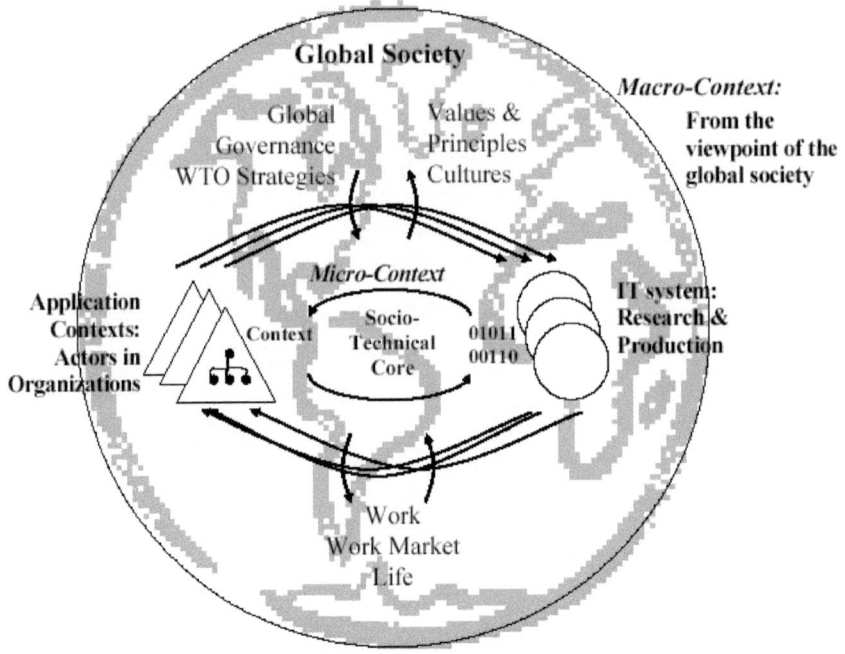

Figure 11: A pictorial representation of the elements of the Mikropolis platform (from Porto &Simon 2007)

In the context of projects for introducing computer systems in organizations, the model describes the use of historical analysis of technological developments based on the theory of path dependency as described in (Schreyögg et al. 2003). The model describes *Technology use paths* that reflect paradigms, guiding principles, standards, methods, products, and tools that were developed in the lifetime of a technology in the society, in organizations and in the technology artifacts. This involves the historical development and establishment process of certain socio-technical structures until reaching their actual state; i.e. the history of the social interactions among the actors that were involved in and affected by the development of a technology, of the actors' conflicts and consequent power losses and wins, and of the guiding principles and the supporting technical paradigms. This historical analysis thus adds value to the previous perspectives by examining the conditions that led to the success or failure of certain alternatives, and enabling one to use them as lessons for future technology development.

4.2.2. The Mikropolis Model in this study

The Mikropolis Model is used in this study as a framework for identifying and analyzing interdependencies from a variety of perspectives when introducing computer systems in organizations. My point of departure is the Mikropolis Model's emphasis of considering prevailing interdependencies between information technology development and usage and between organizational structures and society. **Figure 12** summarizes my understanding of the Mikropolis Model and how I use it in this section as an analytical tool for my work as described here next.

I take the view that a context in society can be curved out as a specific organization or a whole sector under consideration. A conspicuous aspect of any such organization is its management style and practice understood as how people and other resources in the organization are organized to achieve the set organizational goals and objectives. For the health sector, the goals and objectives referred to in this definition are the mandates and responsibilities defined in the laws that govern their activities in the sector. In any organization we have an *organization structure* defining the arrangement of responsibilities, authorities and relationships so that the various actors playing different roles can work in a focused and coordinated way irrespective of specialization differences. For the many tools that they need to achieve their work, one is the use of information technologies – both the hardware and software applications. In an organization such as the health sector there are various information and communication technologies used and not just computer artifacts. A closer inspection in organizations' use of technologies will reveal that the use of these technologies is realized in the backdrop of motivations that touch on how the actors carry out their tasks and therefore have a direct interplay with the organization structure in place. This interaction is especially so when the technology is used more as a managerial multi-tasks support tool as opposed to its use as a purely automation tool.

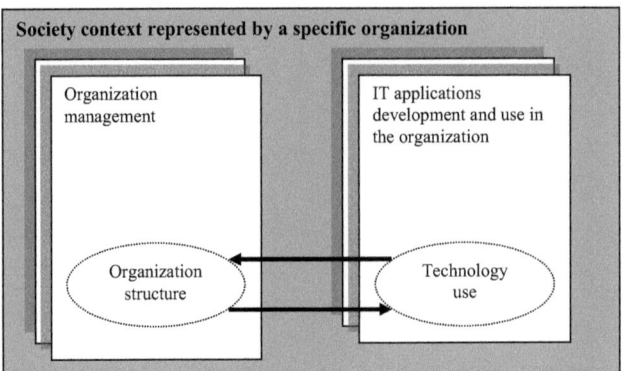

Figure 12: The interrelation of specific organization structure and use of technology

From this adopted view of an organization and the way it's structured I recognize the existence of political aspects in a given organization. As a consequence, when we talk of socio-technical orientation we are especially aware of the sociopolitical contexts in which information technologies are developed, deployed, operated and maintained. This view is directly similar to what Mikropolis Model identifies as the *socio-technical perspective* of technology use in organizations. In Mikropolis this view is explained as the underlying *reciprocity between software development, deployment and the context of usage* (Krause et al. 2006).

As an analytical research tool I use the Mikropolis Model (MM) to provide a framework for identifying and analyzing interdependencies in an organization context (such as the Kenya Health Sector) from two main perspectives: the macro- and micro -perspective. The *macro perspective* focuses on the interrelationships between the organizations that are active in the sector and the larger society in which they are embedded. **Figure** 13 depicts interrelationships of organizations in the sector, with indications of their nature of relations. The inter-organization relations identified here are *partners* and *clients*: *Partners* – with other government ministries, with the development partners and with academic institutions; *clients* representing those who seek public health services (general population).

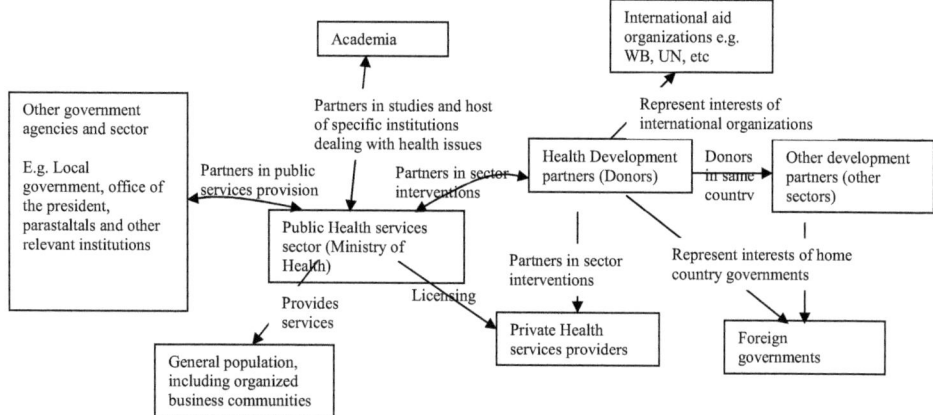

Figure 13: **Health sector macro perspective with indication of collaboration**

The Micro perspective focuses on intra-organization systems relations. I depict the intra-relations in the health sector (specifically public health system) during the course of establishing the hospital information system. I represent the intra-sector organization relations between the four tiers described previously. The Micro level perspective of the elements of networking amongst these levels is depicted in **Figure 14.**

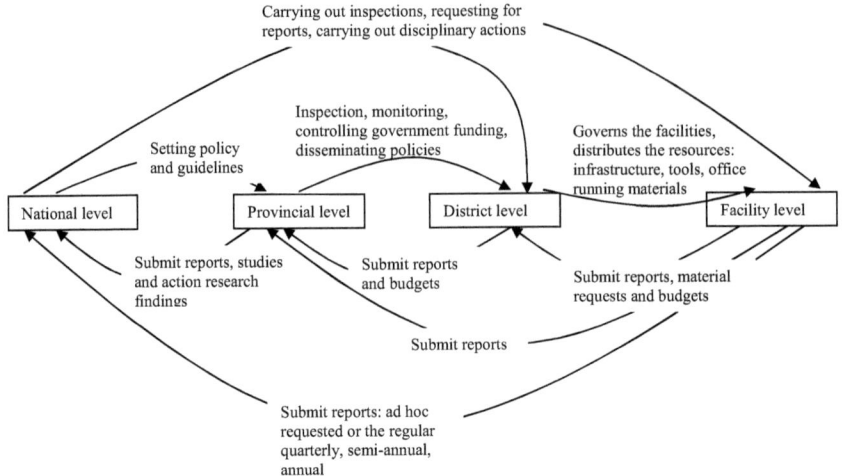

Figure 14: Health sector micro- perspective indicating relations

At this point I have presented a static view of the sector from both the macro – and micro - perspectives. However, the Mikropolis Model goes ahead to support study of socio-technical aspects that are features of introducing computer based systems in organizations. To exploit this Mikropolis Model feature, I borrow the analytical concepts of: stakeholders and technology use path as the axis to plot my understanding of the health sector features.

Stakeholder analysis

As subscribers to the socio-technical view of computer systems, it is relevant to take an analytical view on stakeholders. I understand stakeholders as persons that have or claim ownership rights, or have interests in an organization entity. The interests or claim to rights is to be seen in the person's responsibilities in relation to organization's activities. This is similar to the view advanced by Clarkson (1995) in Kim (2000) in defining stakeholders in corporations. For a definition, the study adopts the definition of stakeholders as advanced by Pouloudi (1997) ... *"the participants [in the development process] together with any other individuals, groups or organizations whose actions can influence or be influenced by the development and use of a system whether directly or indirectly"*. In the spirit of participatory design and development methods of software, identification of project stakeholders is a starting point to bringing them on board and facilitating that they influence not only the process but also the results of projects.

70

Embracing a user-oriented perspective, socio-technical approaches emphasize that thorough insight into the work practices in which IT applications will be used should be the starting point for design and implementation.

The Mikropolis Model concept of stakeholders provides for categories that "... *inform us about the specific abilities, perceptions, and preferences of stakeholders in the intervention. Their specific interests, tasks, activities and the technology used to support them are at the center of the socio-technical system view*" (Simon et al. 2006). These are helpful insights in identifying implicit or explicit differentiating factors of individuals, organization units and whole organizations in the health sector. In this section, I specifically use the Mikropolis Model stakeholder concept for two things:

- Identification of this study's stakeholder categories
- Identification of the tasks and activities that the study stakeholders perform. These are the relevant roles, functions and other comments relating to their being part of the team

Whereas identification of stakeholders and their related tasks come directly from the Mikropolis Model, this study relates the identification to the power relations by making a reference to the nature of relations that the broad categories of stakeholders have. This way for each of the projects providing empirical results, I extend the stakeholder analysis to include an indication of the structure of their relations.

Project 1: Stakeholder analysis

Stakeholder category	Stakeholders	Roles in the project
National level	Chief Health Records and Information Officer, Deputy Chief Health Records and Information Officer	Gave the research permit to work with the health records and information department at the facility. This authorization served as a directive to lower levels to collaborate in the project
Provincial level	Provincial Health Records and Information Officer, deputy provincial Health Records and Information Officer	Gave the green light to carry out the study in their province of jurisdiction. The deputy was a key resource person in the workshops
District level	District medical officer of Health, District Health Records and Information Officer	Directed the facility to collaborate with us for the study. They were resource persons in various activities based on their knowledge of the sector at the district level.
Facility level	Medical Superintendent, Hospital matron, Head of Health Records and Information department, outpatient	The facility hosted the study, the medical superintendent facilitated our presence in the facility (office allocation, staff release to do data

	Health Records and Information officer, inpatient Health Records and Information Officer Health Records and Information Clerks	entry, etc). The health records and information department officers were the direct counterparts in the study and all project activities.

Figure 15: Stakeholder categories and roles

Structure of relations amongst the stakeholders

The national level coordinates and controls the other levels. The relation amongst them is a classical hierarchical organization structure whereby a lower level organization unit reports to the one above it.

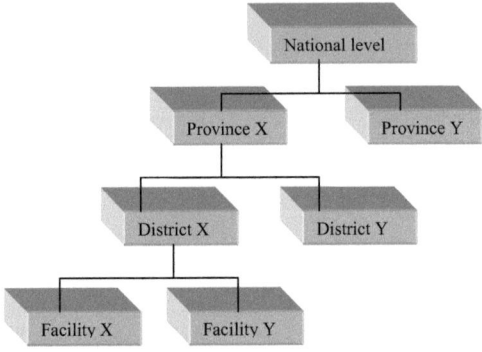

Figure 16: Stakeholders structure

Project 2: Stakeholder analysis

This project falls in the context of health reforms guided by the *Paris declaration on aid effectiveness* (WorldBank 2005). The thrust of the declaration is striving for effectiveness of development assistance especially by aligning the aid to recipient countries' priorities, systems and procedures. It is in this context that the platform was conceived as a partnership project with the ministry of health. The platform was conceptualized as a strategic resource that would increase transparency and access to information in the reforms process. The two stakeholder categories in this project are the government's ministry of health and the health development partners.

Stakeholder category	Stakeholders	Roles in the project
Health Development	World Bank, United Nations	Conceptualized the need for a platform where they

partners	Children and Education Fund (UNICEF), World health Organization (WHO), development agencies from (Denmark, Germany, Japan, UK, France, Italy)	could share the documents amongst themselves and also with the ministry. Needed to get access to ministry documents. Were not comfortable with the restricted information flow and communication problems between them and the ministry
Ministry of Health (MoH)	Health Sector Reform Secretariat, Directorate of e-government	Were to provide the content for the platform: documents, reports and guidelines. Directorate of e-government provided the ICT personnel who was full time at the reform secretariat in the ministry of health

Figure 17: Stakeholders categories and roles

Structure of relations amongst the stakeholders

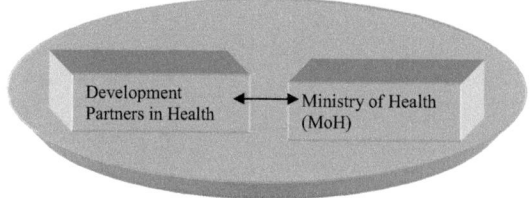

Figure 18: Stakeholder structure

Project 3: Stakeholder analysis

Stakeholder category	Stakeholders	Roles in the project
Faith based organizations	Christian Health Association of Kenya (CHAK), Kenya Episcopal Conference (KEC), Supreme Council of Kenya Muslims, (SUPKEM), Mission for Essential Drugs and Supplies (MEDS)	Representatives were in the technical working group and were producing a lot of knowledge artifacts especially documents that they wanted to capture and a platform to enable easy sharing. Other than documents, they wanted to conveniently document and have access to research results such as policy documents from other countries that had successfully implemented the collaboration between the government and the civil society
Ministry of Health (MoH)	Health care financing department	Represented in the working group by the health care financing experts since the collaboration was to do with the financial allocations to the faith based health service providers
Development partners	development agencies (from Denmark, Germany, UK), the World Bank	With the lead of one development agency that was financing the technical working group, they were interested in having the process documented and the results fed to the wider body of knowledge in the sector towards equitable and wide access to health services in the country.

Figure 19: Stakeholders categories and roles

4.2.2.1. Structure of relations amongst the stakeholders

The ministry licenses the health service providers and does not maintain a close control of their operations in what would be called an organization structure. In principle they form a same level structure where all three interact with each other without the need to use another as a proxy or through a hierarchical relation structure. Each category of stakeholders has direct contact to the others.

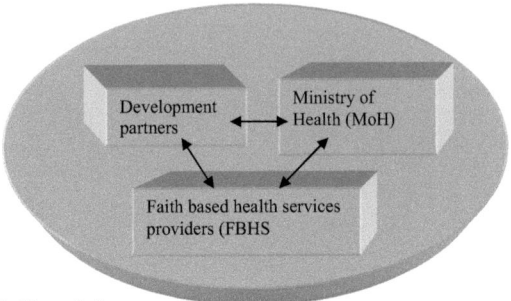

Figure 20: Stakeholders relations

Technology use preparedness in the public health sector

The Mikropolis Model defines *technology use path* as a tool to analyze the history of technology use and respective decisions concerning technology use over time. The analysis of such a history allows identifying stakeholders' technology experiences, power structures leading to particular decisions, and arguments for or against a particular technical option (Simon et al. 2006). In this study I use this concept in a different manner. The concern is the health sector players' background preparedness for IT solutions. The study uses the technology use path concept of the Mikropolis Model to trace IT competencies and experiences which can inform the propensity of embracing IT solutions in the sector. We want to get a view of the current IT use preparedness in each project partner organization. An understanding of these background issues goes a long way to explain the reason for positions and views advanced by stakeholders and therefore their influence in the development efforts and use of technology in the sector.

Technology use path analysis shows that there is a wide difference in the levels of embrace to the use of information and communication technologies in the sector. At the national level, the chief health records and information officer and his deputy were not using any computer. Their secretary had a computer for preparing office memos, typing speeches and other general word-processing tasks. The provincial office had one computer – shared by the provincial head of health records and information and her deputy. This was however non-operational at the time of the study. At the district, the district medical officer of health had a computer that was functional and he was using it to track personnel posting (records of who is working where) in the district as well as for monitoring quality reports in the facilities. The district health records and information officer was based at the hospital where there was one computer. Although filing of the health records was done manually, the reports that the higher tiers asked for from the hospital were summarized with the computer using word processing and spreadsheet applications. There was neither specialized software for medical records management nor a computer operations clerk in the department.

The following are important observations on the technological preparedness in the public health sector as experienced in the project 1:

- Physical infrastructure: By their nature and situation in the developing country, the infrastructure problems are predominantly visible in the sector. The means for communication and general information flow are limited. This limits the extent to which the partners are exposed to new knowledge and access to resources for keeping abreast with technological advances. Again limits their ability to conceptualize what solutions exist to address their problems. Budgetary allocations to provide enabling technical environment take secondary priority in the sector.
- Technical capacity: The levels of information technology education and experience are a limiting factor in the health sector. Whereas there is a course on health records and information management at the Kenya Medical Training College, other hands - on skills and experiences needed to master and gain proficiency in the technologies are generally missing.
- Staffing problems: There are fewer health records and information officers compared to other represented functions in the sector. This has the consequence of poor data collection, work overload that limits the opportunities for staff to reflect, critique, develop and adopt appropriate tools for data collection and adaptation.

- Remuneration problems: Project establishment meetings are seen as opportunities for earning an extra pay with the focus shifting from meetings' results to short term monetary gains by participants. These meetings can have poor attendance if there are questions about the availability of attendance allowances.
- Cross - pollination of experiences and skills: Staff lack exposure and forums to exchange skills and experiences across other (advanced) organizations, sectors, opportunities for on - job training and continued professional development courses while at work. This has meant the staff have not updated their skills and collected more experiences that would greatly enhance their abilities and technology use proficiency.
- Isolated islands of excellence: Whereas donors, non - public health service providers are drowning in abundance and comfort of IT infrastructure (such as high -speed interconnectivity) the bulk of the sector represented by the public providers operates in abject lack.

4.3. ANT as an analytical tool to my work

An interesting approach to conceptualize the social, technical and natural contexts in which project establishment takes place is provided by the so-called Actor-Network Theory (ANT), sometimes also referred as sociology of translation. ANT is a theory coming from science and technology studies whose foundational works can be found in (Callon 1986a, 1986b; Latour 1987, 1988; Law 1988, 1991). ANT suggests a socio-technical account in which neither social nor technical positions are privileged over the other, regarding the "world" as heterogeneous and seeking to identify the strength or weakness of the interrelations between the elements. By letting technical interests remain in the background, the concern of ANT can be understood as getting to appraise the context. Systemic view of network elements where each actor is itself also a simplified network helps to identify and understand the interests, attitudes and perceptions held by the stakeholders. According to Boudourides (2001) ... *processes of socio-technical development occur in a series of negotiations among the involved actors (to recall Latour's famous slogan "follow the actors"). Aligned actors construct and maintain a network by enrolling allies, mobilizing resources and translating interests. In this sense, translations are understood as the actors' activities of ongoing negotiations, which define actors' physiognomy and the relations among themselves, "their identity, the roles they should play, the nature of bonds that unite them, their respective size and the history"* (Callon 1986a, p. 24).

According to ANT a socio-technical account privileges neither social nor technical positions; it's about network elements and their interconnections. This means ANT recognizes the relations in a heterogeneous network to be full of a hybrid of entities as opposed to purely technical or purely social relations. The concern in ANT is network strength or weakness resulting from alliances built up by the network elements. The various stakeholders and actors in the health sector context form various networks whose interconnections uniquely define the health sector. Therefore for this study ANT is relevant in the identification and analysis of the network features, how the actors assume identities according to the prevailing context and adapt their interactions to achieve their own background interests and goals. These goals and interests go beyond the defined mandates of the sector players by virtue of being part of the health sector. In this section I will extend the static representation of the sector players (whose identification has been facilitated by Mikropolis) to analyze the strengths of linkages between them.

ANT has features that make it a useful lens for analysis in this study. These follow from its sociological background and its use to study not only existing but also emerging networks of actors over time. I specifically use it to achieve two things: *to open up the health sector "black-box"* and *to relate the value of our approaches as support to project establishment experiences.*

- *To open up the health sector "black-box".* The sector is comprised internally of a myriad of networks and interrelations which are not explicit for someone from outside. One wishing to learn how the sector operates for the purpose of establishing a project needs to open up the "black-box". ANT's strong feature of not only studying how networks are formed but also systematically opening up networks to bring out the features holding the network intact come in handy here. This study does not attempt to open up all health sector networks but only depict the relevant ones whose features relate to the study results. A special network feature of interest to us is the finding out of which actors have what power in specific networks and their influence thereof. From a reflection of these power positions amongst the actors, then it's clear which relations must be addressed to

stabilize or form a network. This study's proposed steps are specifically meant to facilitate this.
- *To explain and relate the value of our approaches as support to project establishment experiences.* ANT's moments of problematization, interessment, enrollment and mobilization in (Callon 1986a) are understood as the results of this study's propositions. This is a consequence of viewing a successful project establishment undertaking as the establishment of a project "black-box" with its own fulfilled conditions to hold it together and forge ahead with the project. Whereas the achievement of the above moments in ANT are discussed later in this study, in this section we lay the foundation by identifying network forming points and important linkages needed to be strengthened.

4.3.1. Identification of Actor issues, goals and relational structures in case projects

The systematic process of using ANT for analysis as proposed by Callon (1986a) is one that progresses in two steps:
- Identification of the issues of each actor that are problematic to the project at hand
- Identification of the goals that actors bring in and therefore influence their ability and willingness to cooperate in the project by shaping their positions in the network.

We shall extend these steps to include a third analysis step of summarizing the relation strengths. The argument is that for a successful project establishment, it is necessary that the power differences so identified need to be negotiated and addressed as part of project establishment activities.

4.3.1.1. Project 1: Actor issues and goals

The actors that can be identified as participating in the interactions are: the representatives of the national level, the district level and the facility (hospital) level. We identify the issues coming out in the interaction for each of these actors and the associated goals for each.

Issues		
National level	*District Level*	*Facility Level*
- Maintaining the status quo and ability to exert authority - Insistence on processes than results with the consequence that things should be done as they have always been done	- Struggling to align problems in their jurisdictions with the demands and guidelines from the headquarters	- Unsupportive higher level leading to poor facilitation of their needs to provide services
Goals/interests		
National level	*District Level*	*Facility Level*
• To be seen to oversee a functional health system by getting information from the low cadres in the ministry hierarchy when and as they need it	• Better fulfillment of demands from the national level while sustaining a working health system through better overview of the jurisdiction dynamics especially via improved supervisory roles	• Better tools for surveillance especially in tracking outbreaks and thereby achieving better and timely reporting as demanded by the higher levels

Figure 21: Project 1 actors' issues and goals

An attempt is made here to network the degrees of power relations that exist between the groups of the stakeholders identified above.

Note:		National	Provincial	District	Facility
- 1: denotes a medium power intensity relation and - 2: denotes a high power intensity relation between any two specified actors.	National	-	1	2	2
	Provincial	0 (-1)	-	1	2
	District	0 (-2)	0 (-2)	-	1
	Facility	0 (-2)	0 (-2)	0 (-1)	-

Figure 22: Matrix of actor power strengths

Highlights of power relations

	Link	Evaluation of link strength	Explanation / Description
1	National --> Provincial	Medium	- Direct supervisor relation especially communicating policies and guidelines from the national level to the provincial level
	Provincial --> National	Weak	
2	National -->District	Strong	- A national level interaction with the district is understood as an indication of problems in the region. Interaction is initiated from national level
	District--> National	Weak	
3	National --> facility	Strong	- National level interventions are understood as corrective or punitive measures. Interventions are initiated from the national level and there is no initiation for a report or tools improvement from the facility
	Facility --> National	Weak	
4	Provincial --> District	Medium	- Direct supervisor relation. Seldom is there initiation of collaboration engagements from the district such as presentation of plans and budgets
	District--> provincial	Weak	
5	Provincial --> Facility	Strong	- Provincial level interventions are understood as the representing the national level and therefore similar to relation between national and facility.
	Facility --> provincial	Medium	
6	District --> facility	Medium	- Direct supervisor relation, always understood as a better facilitator than the provincial and national levels whose missions are either directives or corrections - Requests don't start from the facility to the district level, but from district requesting information from the facilities or providing mechanisms to operate the facility
	Facility -->district	Weak	

Figure 23: project 1 highlight of actor power relations

4.3.1.2. Project 2: Actor issues and goals

In this project the two categories of actors identified as participating in the interactions are: the health development partners group and the ministry of health. We identify the issues coming out in the interaction for each of these actors and the associated goals for each.

Issues	
Development partners	Ministry of Health
- Concerns over ministry's commitment to collaborate and share reform documents	- Control, authority and ownership of sector reform documents
Goals/interests	
Development partners	Ministry of health
• Having access to documents in a more transparent process of documents sharing	• Sharing the documents and policies in ways that don't compromise their control and ownership

The two as equal partners represent fairly equal strength characterization of power relations between the two organizations.

4.3.1.3. Project 3: Actor issues and goals

In this project the three broad categories of actors identified as participating in the interactions are: the health development partners group, the faith - based health services providers and the ministry of health. We identify the issues and the associated goals coming out in the interaction for each of these actors.

Issues		
Development partners	Ministry of Health	Faith- based health services providers
- Concerns over establishment of collaboration	- Control, authority and ownership of documents from the technical working group	- Not to fall victim as earlier endeavors that failed and left no documentation
Goals/interests		
Development partners	Ministry of Health	Faith - based health services providers
• Having an open and transparent platform to share documents and other experiences	• Having access to information produced in the working group	• Maintain a record of all efforts, facilitate learning and sharing information transparently

The three as equal partners represent fairly equal - strength characterization of power relations between the organizations.

4.4. Beyond obsession with power structures: interaction-moments in actor networks

In the previous sections I have discussed the Kenya health sector composition, hierarchical organizational structure and indicated the power structures that are in place. I have attributed the power intensity experienced in the empirical projects to the way the sector is structured. I have shown the static networks in the sector and how the various actors and stakeholders relate to each other. Using the theories of Mikropolis and the actor network theory (ANT), I have shown the power relations experienced in my project establishment cases and argued that these relations draw influence from the chains of command and information flow in constituent organizational units. In the following sections of the chapter I continue the analysis of the cases but in a deeper way by zeroing in on interaction details in the course of the projects. Whereas the analysis results presented before can be described as *a vertical analysis of sector stakeholders' relations*, in these sections of the chapter I take *a horizontal view to bring out interaction details* across represented organizations in my projects. Making a horizontal slice of the project stakeholders' relations, I get an entry point to discuss specific project experiences that bring out aspects of such interactions.

The motivation for this deeper view of the project contexts is to highlight the intricate realities of carrying out projects in contexts beset by the presented power structures. The gloomy picture of the inhibitive characteristics of power structures should not be understood as argument against successful implementation of projects carried out with participation of all users across the organization structures. The proposition made here is the argument that the engagement needs to take a different approach, deviating from traditional Scandinavian approaches that only worked with the *shop-floor level* workers by collaborating with their trade unions, thus failing to infiltrate the whole organization structure. I argue for a holistic approach that cuts across all organization levels and promotes interactions across organizations and organization units. However, the rationale for embracing participatory design remains unchanged –recognition of the symbiotic relationship between human activities and technical systems (such as information systems).

4.4.1. Symbiotic relation: human activities and technical systems

Participatory Design (PD) practice is based on the recognition that computer systems (as technology artifacts) exist in a relationship with human actors in their daily life experiences. Such systems find their reason to be from the human activities that they support. It is this symbiotic relationship between technology (such as computer systems) and the daily human activities in the course of their work that informs the motivation to align technical interventions to the actual realities of human activities in organizational settings. Participatory design practitioners act not only in recognition but also in promotion of better relationships between technology and human activities in their work. Suchman (1993, p. viii) summarizes this relation by arguing that researchers with interest in PD are centrally concerned " ... *with a more humane, creative, and effective relationship between those involved in technology's design and its use, and in that way between technology and the human activities that provide technological systems with their reason for being"*. Human activities are organized in specific ways with various levels of authority and responsibility defined as organizational structures.

This study takes the specific position that the power structures in an organization are directly informed by the way the workforce is organized. This consequently leads to human characteristics that work against smooth symbiotic relationships between their activities and technologies. The manifestation of friction is in terms of questions of power and quest for democratic space at the workplace (cf. Kanstrup 2003). These issues will progress into project settings that are formed by workforce coming from such scenarios. From different power positions, participants in a project bring distinct interests and objectives with varying views concerning the role of technology in the organization. These were my experiences in the empirical case studies. From a perspective of context specific power positions and issues of democratic spaces at work, I am proposing contextualization of methodological approaches that are used to introduce technology in such contexts. Without losing sight of the power problems I argue for a holistic approach traversing organizational structures in a bid to identify and negotiate the causes of friction in collaborative human activities beyond the prevalent power structures. The key is to bring up a dialog that operates above the gloom of power structures. The methodologies applicable are enriched to defuse issues of power and tame the effects arising from such issues.

4.4.2. Holistic approaches traversing organizational structures to defuse power issues

Initial participatory design projects targeted specific concerns between worker unions and technology introductions mainly with the aim to ensure participation of union members in decisions about technology that touched on their work activities. This was based on the strong industrial democracy in Scandinavia seeking to empower workers and safeguard their interests against technological interventions reinforcing already existing power structures. Such reinforcement can be viewed in terms of systems being introduced as tools of management to exercise control that favors management's goals and strategies. Political considerations arise as a result of technology introduction that workers see as bringing in *deletious effects, dislocations and deskilling of workers* (Kensing & Blomberg 1998: p. 169) while the systems are promoted to address issues of productivity and efficiency (a view advanced by higher management levels in an organization). Interventions that target whole organization hierarchies and not solely a given level of the hierarchy promote the diffusion of participatory ideals in a wider organizational context as these ideals become resources of action for technology design professionals and as reorientation guide for managers' courses of action in ways that take into account interests from all levels. I call the approach resulting from this view a ***holistic approach*** whose motivation is to address political considerations arising from interests such as search for democratic spaces at work or the strive for productivity and efficiency in organizations as far as technical systems are concerned. I use the term political here to denote the aspects of internal conflicting interrelationships (cf. Beck 2002).

This situates my discussion to a contention between parts of structural hierarchies in workforce organization and by extension raising questions of how to address prevailing distribution of power in organizations. By promoting workers' participation in the design of technologies that affected their lives, later Scandinavian projects sought to "... *rebalance the power relations between users and technical experts and between workers and managers* (Kensing & Blomberg 1998, 181). Bringing the representatives of these structure levels in the context of a participatory informed project brings out such negative influences of power differences as silencing others or making themreluctant to honestly express views. I propose that these influences can be addressed by methodological approaches whose origin is informed from interventions that take a holistic view of human activities in organizations.

The way to such an approach in a project process is to facilitate engagements and involvement of participants above the ever present power processes. In a project setting, I start from situating the participants in their default settings which I refer to as organization arenas. This makes sense since all project participants will identify themselves with an organization or affiliation to a similar group (**Figure 24**). This means these arenas are static with life spans that are not limited to a project's life cycle.

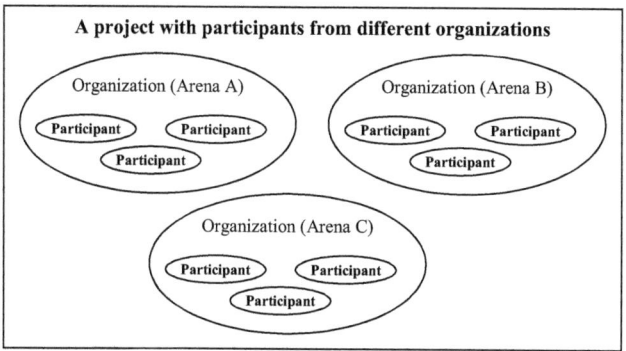

Figure 24: Static organizational arenas of project participants

4.4.3. Interaction-Moments

As the project gets under way, what results is the building of alliances and supra - networks that defy organizational boundaries. The project settings and associated goals cut across the organization based arenas. The participants taking part form networks of associations that according to ANT are represented as networks of actors. The manifestations of the formation of these networks are in the interactions taking place to exchange both tangible and intangible artifacts. The interactions in the course of a collaboration project involving several partners (both organizational and individual) are many taking different features, covering varying issues that are simultaneously handled by the networks of actors. I introduce the term *"interaction-moments"* to refer to the distinguishable features of the interactions at specific points in time during the interactions across organizational arenas. **Figure 25** shows a presentation of the virtual project arena in which interaction-moments occur.

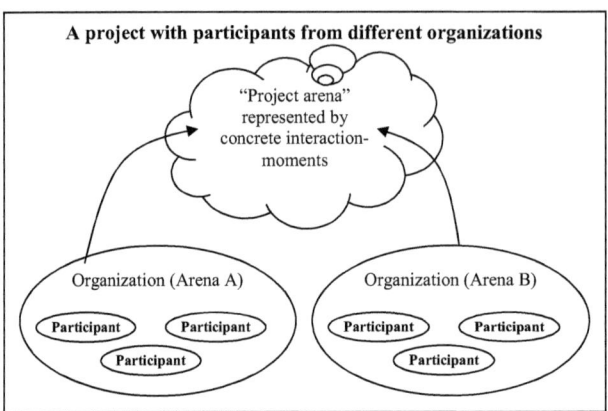

Figure 25: Project interactions beyond the organizational arenas

The process of identifying the interaction-moments requires analysis of interactions in a network with an approach that looks simultaneously into *the identity of the actors* involved and into *the content of the interactions*. The content is not limited to the products of interaction but also those aspects of actors that they bring to the interactions in the course of the projects. Actor aspects are generally their interests, concerns, goals, and responsibilities arising from of their daily work activities. The identity, content and product aspects of collaboration networks give such networks their existence by being responsible for not only the stimulation of the network action but also its sustenance. Leaving the power questions of interaction in the background, I am interested in highlighting the defining aspects of the interactions that I see existing in parallel to the power structures and chains of command. The interactions are manifestations of forming relations amongst the actors in the course of project related tasks. These are actor networks comprised of actors across organizational boundaries and whose interaction details can be specifically identified as touching on issues that contribute to the progress of the collaboration between organizations and individual actors taking part.

Without losing sight of our awareness of the actors (identities that they bring to a project setting), I go further and make a categorization of the concerns and issues forming the bulk of the interactions to what I call *"interaction-moments"*. Specifically I identify *managerial, professional and technical* interaction-moments that reflect the main aspects of discussions at defined points in time during their engagements. These are not actor groupings as a result of their positions in the respective organizations but rather the features (noticeable aspects) of the kind of relationships that emerge in the actors' interactions. These form the raison d'être of the relations that evolve amongst the various project actors. The recognition of these aspects and facilitation to address the underlying concerns becomes the challenge of securing and sustaining commitment to information systems projects. I understand the underlying concerns that come in the interaction-moments as questions of collaboration, project - team formation and the project process. The participating actors are anchored 'somewhere' that I generally refer to as an organization context which serves to influence identities. *An organization as an entity is not neutral since it represents something and provides its actors therefore with a view from somewhere* (Gärtner & Wagner (1996)). I understand "view" to represent an influence on their identities that they bring in a network. For example, in an organization actors have roles, especially as defined by their expertise, skills and responsibilities (positions in respective organizations) that give them an identity. This identity will always be at the background influencing their views in projects.

In an engagement the actors' interactions are influenced by the identities they draw from respective contexts. My choice of names for the interaction-moments is as used in project management discourse on division of labor where the general meanings of the terms (managerial, professional, technical) hint on the subject and content of corresponding interaction-moments. The interaction features in a given interaction-moment should not be viewed as determined by the professional responsibility (job titles and positions) of the actors. By this I mean, it is not the case that managers are excluded from technical interaction-moments. In a managerial interaction-moment, there can be design experts involved, only that the concern of the discussion at that point in time can be generally picked up as being of a managerial nature. Consequently, it is not unusual to have a single actor participating in all the various interaction-moments. As an example, a professional systems designer carrying out an Information System (IS) project in a developing country with shortage of experts will be participating in managerial project management issues as well as technical implementation details and tasks. Such problems of supply in terms of professional experts in developing country contexts were also identified by Biru (2008).

It follows from this discussion that a project is established and run within an evolving network of actors whose interactions hint at concerns that need to be addressed for the network to form and stabilize. The aspects and concerns are rooted in the context of the actors, such as the health sector in the cases I studied.

Below I present an overview of the interaction-moments from my empirical data of two projects in the heath sector. These are meant to demonstrate how I have come up with this idea. Interaction-moments are results of a reflective close analysis of daily interactions in the course of establishing the projects.

4.4.3.1. Project 1: Hospital information system at "Hillside" General Hospital

The organizational arenas in the project are: ministerial headquarters (departments of heath records and management information systems), provincial administration office (specifically health records staff), district administration office (the health management team), "Hillside" provincial hospital and the technical development team. **Figure 26** demonstrates the marked interactions amongst the various actors from each arena in the project interaction space.

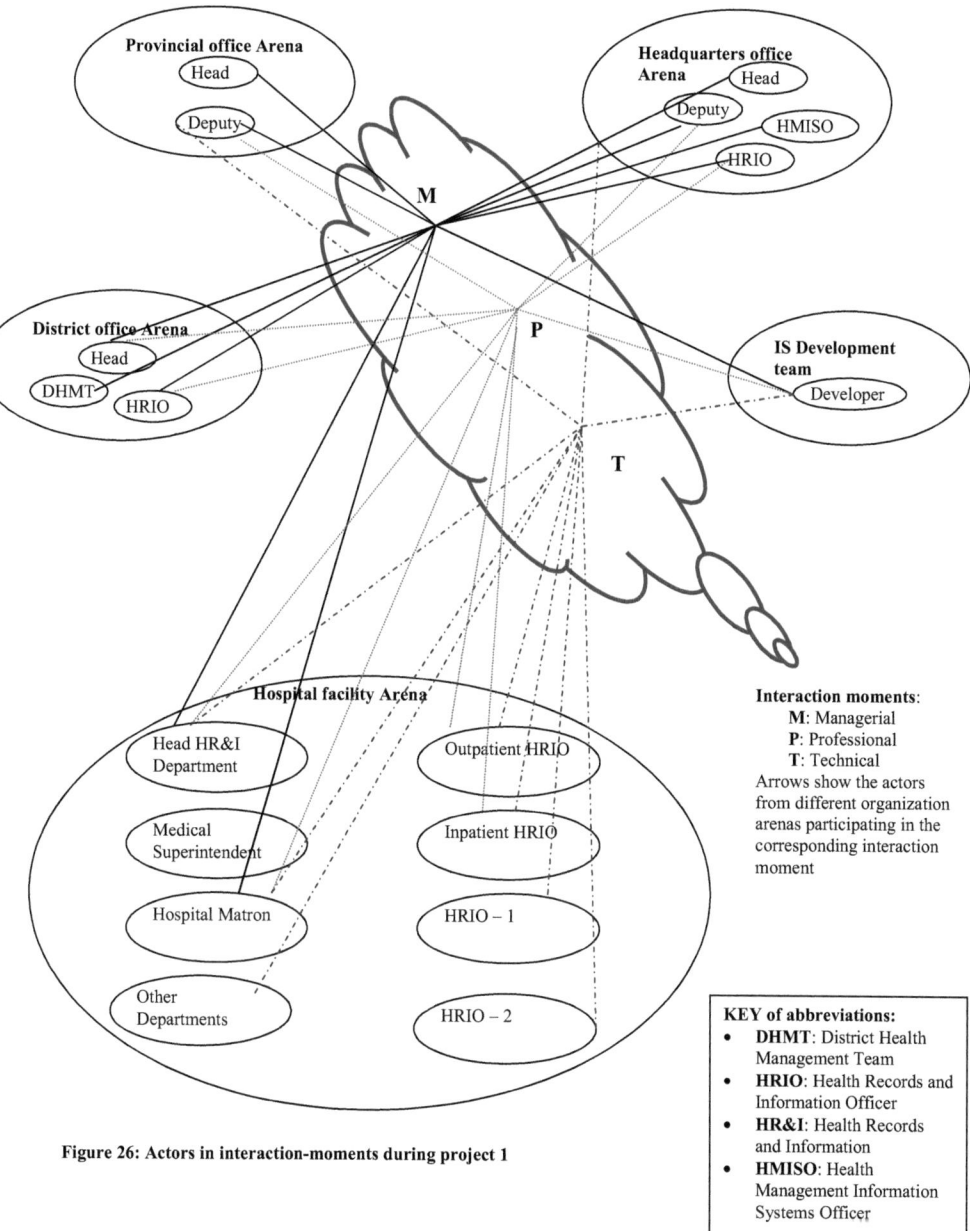

Figure 26: Actors in interaction-moments during project 1

4.4.3.2. Project 2: Platform for storing and sharing health sector reform documents

The organization arenas are: the members of the health donor working group, a development agent and the ministry headquarters (health reforms secretariat). The **Figure 27** depicts the actors from each organizational arena identified to be taking part in the interaction-moments.

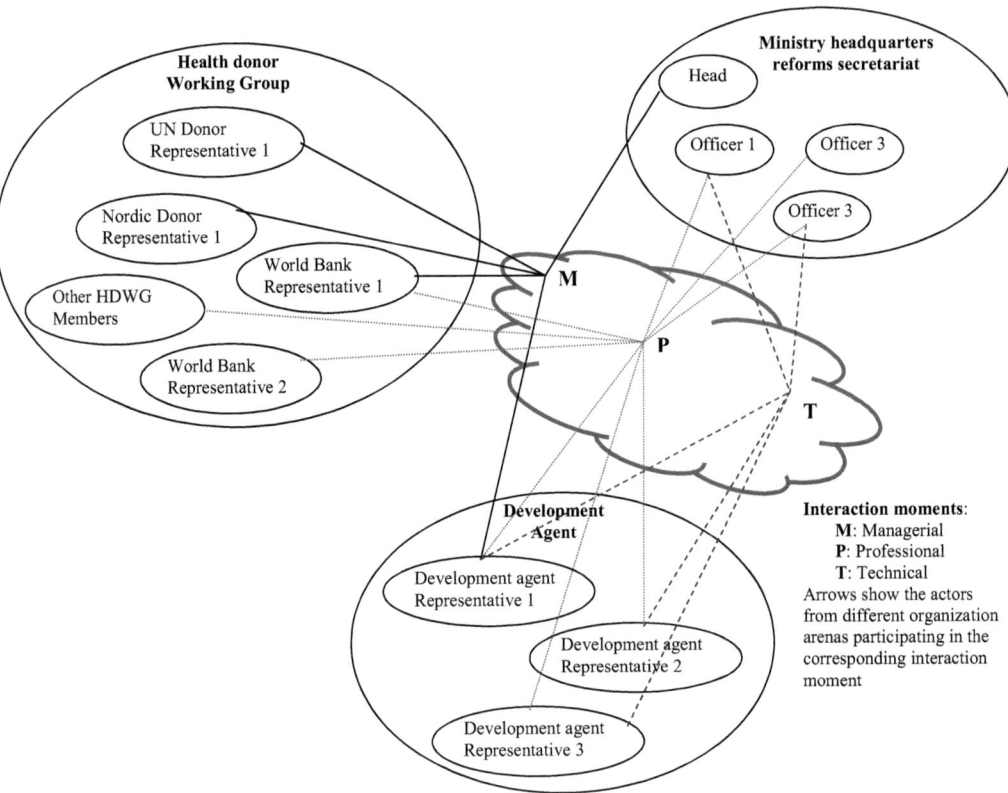

Figure 27: Actors in interaction-moments during project 2

4.4.4. Summary of Interaction-Moments

In the following table I concretize the concept of interaction moments by making a detailed description of the features that are used to identify them during project engagements. For each I also present techniques and strategies that are applicable during each interaction moment with observation that a practitioner needs to be aware of. This table is aimed at making it clear how the above described interaction moments during the projects were identified.

Technical interaction-moments	
Addresses issues about concrete, specific project results	
Features	- Involves high levels of information and attention to details - High risks emanating from context specific issues but reduced by the fact that the scope is defined by other interaction-moments
Involves discussions on	- Specific technical issues: e.g. choice of technology - Project process issues: e.g. detailed schedule of activities - Realization issues: e.g. process automations, presentation/interface decisions
Techniques and strategies	- One-to-one interactions: e.g. workshops, interviews - Activities: e.g. assignments, reporting/presentation and prototyping - Building relationships: e.g. relaxing bureaucratic rules, direct conflict resolution, building empathy, defining relationship boundaries
Observations	- Important that the actors' availability is relatively stable. High turnover will delay agreements and production of improved artifacts - Achieved resonance is not transferable

Professional interaction-moments	
Discusses issues targeted at common understanding and focusing of goals to project targets and objectives. The objective is to develop commonly shared blue prints that will map the problem to a solution.	
Features	- High levels of information and flexibility from issues external to the project - Innovation: Hitherto stable patterns in the work activities and organizational functioning processes are questioned
Involves discussions on	- Organizational issues: redefinition of general conditions of work, organizational and larger political contexts, redefinition of objectives - Project processes: e.g. responsibilities of collaborating organizations, resource mobilization, monitoring and evaluation
Techniques and strategies	- Promoting professional freedom to interact: e.g. brainstorming features - Instituting or referencing formal procedures: e.g. due process steps to be followed when in contention, reference to authoritative (previously agreed upon) sources - Relaxation of rules to respect individual roles and to allow flexible responsiveness as conditions change
Observations	- Type of actors: representatives of a function in an organization (e.g. head of some team) - Can accommodate turn over better than other moments. Artifacts are produced where competencies are formalized making it easier to easily transfer the moment's achievements - Has affluent property: Issues are forwarded here from other moments

Managerial interaction-moments	
Addresses the broad (collaboration) agreements and other supra-project overarching goals	
Features	- Political engagement of negotiations between organization or amongst organization units, setting global norms of engagement - Proactive (initiating, re-orienting and abstracting project processes and other moments)
Involves discussions on	- Broader rationale of the project - How project relates to and is influenced by other interests: accommodation of external objectives
Techniques and strategies	- Committees and working groups, consultancy intermediaries that blur out philosophical organizational positions (entrenched attitudes) - Building relationships between organizations through informal and formal exchanges
Observations	- Is anchored and influenced by organizational perspectives and philosophical directions - Delegation and responsiveness to other moments keeps the project establishment activities going - Is affected by turnover of participating staff. Established managerial relations, or good organizational relations enable circumventing bureaucracies and formalities

4.5. Conclusions

4.5.1. Reflections on interaction-moments

My analysis points at the importance of understanding interaction features amongst the actors in a network formed by the project team. This helps bring out the underlying issues that act as undercurrents against the efforts to form stable actor networks. Identification of interaction-moments will act as an entry point to identify interests, concerns, individual and organizational goals as well as other influences that cause frictions in an actor network. The categorization of the interactions can be used to inform corrective measures such as the identification of an area of competence to be strengthened by way of changing project team composition. In analyzing specific interaction-moments, it is possible to identify issues that are beyond the scope of the project and better understand the constraints within which the project gets established. The techniques and strategies I have identified as applicable in the different interaction-moments are propositions drawn from my experiences which can inform a methodological approach in similar projects.

Analysis of interaction-moments helps formulate appropriate strategies, an example of which is having consultative briefing of managers from other interaction-moments and facilitating inputs that cut cross the interaction-moments in workshops. They call for recognizing the moments (sometimes in as single setting and concurrently) and then engaging appropriate negotiation (or conflict resolution) techniques to counter frictions. The objective of such negotiation in an interaction-moment is not necessarily to solve the underlying internal differences but to bring to the fore these differences. The achievement of "common-negotiated agreement" in the interaction-moments is necessary for a project establishment undertaking to be considered successful (I later call this achievement of resonance). Whereas this can be achieved to different degrees in different interaction-moments, later problems in the project or project failure can be analyzed against results of interaction-moments. Strong relation as a result of well-handled interaction-moments makes a powerful case for a project as it reinforces the notion of experiencing mutual understanding based on availability of avenues to resolve conflicts.

4.5.2. Interaction-moments as handles to defuse power effects in projects interactions

Whereas I have argued that in the course of project establishment it is possible to distinguish between the three forms of interaction-moments, these moments occur concurrently and simultaneously in the course of a project. The project is defined by the interaction-moments that have a similar characteristic of having defined start and end time, as opposed to organizations that are stable and structured entities. I abstract the project network in terms of the relationships between the issues raised in the three interaction-moments. Conflicts and other problems in the project can be traced back to one or several interaction-moments. I propose two possible scenarios in the way the interaction-moments can relate to one another and therefore influence the results of the stability of the resulting network of project actors.
- The interaction-moments have undefined relations when the boundaries between the moments (issues, identities and products) are conspicuously prevalent. The differentiating factors (i.e. features deemed critical at one moment) are radically different from those of the other moments. Points of intersection of the moments are only noticeable as conflict resolution. Power wielding actors remain engrossed in the power defined by the organizational structures and are seen to intervene in issues that are not from their domain of expertise. Conflict resolution takes over as opposed to having active cooperation amongst the

project actors in forming a stable network as a result of the project establishment activities. The exercise of project establishment gets fragmented with many meetings characterized by the resignation to passively await decisions from others. Different 'languages' get noticed in the interactions with less and less understanding between the participants in the different interaction-moments. The power effects that come along in the context serve only to make the boundaries between the interaction-moments 'thick' to the extent that friction is experienced in discussions cutting across the moments. Issues from one moment are understood as conflicts to the issues being fronted from another moment. The result is that the project establishment network is unstable and the establishment exercise is likely to fail.

- Interaction-moments are characterized by blurred boundaries between the moments. The issues from one moment serve to support the other moment's issues such that the transitions of discussions between moments are transparently experienced in a discussion. The meetings in which the various interaction-moments take place are more of a reflective nature (its clear what is expected from the actors) than of conflict resolution whereby it is about expected differences (conflicts) coming out. There is high flexibility in switching moments, delegation and direction of questions or the solutions to raised issues is noticeable as different expert groups in the network are tasked to find solutions that relate/affect them and hence in those domain areas where they are experts and best placed to find or suggest solutions. Interaction-moments feed each other with the result that the networks of actors form and stabilize as the project gets established. This is the desired scenario in project establishment.

4.5.3. Benefits of taking a holistic organization structure participation

Faced with a context characterized by intensive power relations, I have argued for focusing on interactions that the project team has in their attempts to realize the project. In a context that is as wide as a whole public health sector, the interactions span across organizations and organizational units. As much as there will be the temptation to focus on the 'strong points' in the power structures, I propose that the focus should facilitate interaction of actors from 'weak points' as well. A holistic approach to engage in the whole spectrum of the power structures that are reinforced by the organization structure will provide an entry point to map human activities to technical interventions. There are far reaching advantages to this, two of which are (i.) alignment of technological systems intervention to actual work politics and (ii.) increased potential for sustainability of the project results.

i). By relating technological interventions to the actual realities of work across the organization structure, staff at all levels in the organization structure have an opportunity to learn the everyday work aspects (and detailed workplace arrangements) of the others. In a project setting, this learning is important to the technology experts and consultants taking part in the project establishment. The rationale advanced for introducing technological interventions is to some extent abstract but through support for alignment of the interventions it becomes specific, clear and practical across the staff irrespective of whether it is those that are responsible for administrative aspects or those responsible for the actual work itself. E.g. in our case, without this view, we found that the introduction of a collaborative system as a technical solution for reporting was initially understood as politically as the workers hitherto view reporting as a "service to the top management at the headquarters". Through a holistic involvement across the organization structure, it was possible to address political issues that come to play in the daily work activities. A consequence is that new views about technological interventions emerge; including formation of new networks of collaboration at work (or existing ones being recognized) and strengthened in the organization. This is an observation similar to Tonnessen's (2005) argument that companies have a much wider potential to benefit from innovation through company - wide employee participation as opposed to *"shop floor level participation"*.

ii). A holistic engagement across the whole spectrum of the organization structure has the potential to enhance the organization-wide diffusion and retention of the results. Top levels of staff with managerial and administrative responsibilities have a wider view of the organization scope that facilitates identification of opportunities for replication of results across functional and geographical distributions. In our cases, we have noticed a facilitation of diffusing the results from projects to the whole health sector. In project one, its is clear that the administrators overseeing the public health system at the ministry headquarters have a better view and potential to replicate results than a staff at a busy middle level hospital whose daily work can only be described as hectic. In the other projects, the top management was able to facilitate the adoption of similar projects to support the other stakeholders in their collaboration efforts – the sharing of documents and other knowledge artifacts produced during the sector reforms was not a preserve of the donors and the government officials. This means projects conceived as simple pilot projects have the potential to graduate to sector-wide projects with the consequence that promoted and learned practices get sustained beyond the limited project life cycles.

4.5.4. Evaluation of using ANT as an analysis tool

Using the actor network model to analyze empirical experiences has helped to position actors engaged in the projects within a larger context of the health sector and reflect on their specific contributions in the network through interactions in the existing static networks and those networks attributed to project activities. This helps to reflectively formulate appropriate strategies for effective engagement and interaction amongst the actors. These are informed by reflecting on their interests and goals thus bringing about better formulation of appropriate practices of negotiation in networks formation and evolution. As a researcher it is striking in an actor-network informed analysis to become aware of one's position within a larger context made up of evolving actor networks with interaction-moments that reflect relations between the actors. The unfolding of (un)successful scenarios helps to engage methodological approaches that promote successful project establishment.

5. Critical Reflections from Project Experiences

The results of this study are validated by my experiences in projects done in the Kenyan Health sector. From these experiences, qualitative information forming the basis for the reflections on the implicit context knowledge, is only accessible through real life experiences in the sector. In the appendices I have summarized highlights from the experiences. In this chapter, I pick on specific issues from the description of experiences in the project stories. I further highlight the methodological actions taken in response to the issues encountered. From systematic awareness and dealing with the issues, the experiences with project establishment have improved over projects. From an initial failure based on assumptions as to the specific contextual realities in the sector, project establishment is smooth with fewer disagreements and also taking less time. This is attributed to the systematic managing of those unspoken and unwritten issues informing the project stakeholders' reception of the project.

By spending time and getting exposed for the first time to the working situation in the health sector, I collected rich experiences that the case stories description highlights. My reflection identifies the following issues as being the differentiating factors that I argue are consistent features of the Kenyan health sector context. For each, I describe its understanding and then make references to the case story highlighting the incidences that depict the occurrence of the issues.

5.1. A culture of intensive power relations supported by the organization structure

Various incidences in the interactions highlight that the relations between the staff in the sector are influenced by the 'levels of authority'. Levels of authority, referred to as cadres or job groups in the sector, are defined in the organization hierarchy of the health sector. The authority that comes with the office occupied influences the relations that one staff has with the others either in the same cadre, in a cadre below or in one above in the organization hierarchy. The highlights from the case story that depict this issue include:

Getting the research permit in project 1

At the beginning of the engagement at the Hillside hospital, it was necessary that I get a research permit from the headquarters of the ministry. Whereas this is normal practice for the research in the sector, the process exposed power imbalances in the relations between the tiers in the ministry hierarchy. I find the fact that there was limitation in the help I got from either at the facility or the district and the provincial health administrative offices as an indication of how highly the hierarchical organization structure is stressed. Moreover, the permit was issued without any consultations to the target district where the study was taking place. It means that while at the district the staffs said they can't help with the permit, at the headquarters they were implying that if they are convinced the study is good and relevant; it must be relevant for the district as well, obliging the latter to cooperate in the study.

Composition of the project teams

In the deliberations of who should be included in the project team, it was required that the district health management team (DHMT) – comprised of district level managers – must be included. The push for their inclusion was not for the purposes of sanctioning the project. It was because the design and propositions would not be honored unless the managers were seen to take part. Contrary to emphasis being placed on the actual staff who executed the daily work (work processes), the emphasis was being placed on the managers describing what ought to be done. The issue is further evident in the top-down planning where the managers are said to have attempted to introduce the interconnectivity project but failed to understand the actual demands 'on the ground' and the preparedness of the hospital departments for the interconnection project.

Consultations in resource planning

With the introduction of the cost sharing (Bedi et al. 2003) scheme in Kenya, the facilities have their own funds collected via the fees for registration and issuance of patient cards. The expectation is that the planning for these will be done participatively as a means of resolving some of the problems at the facilities. However, the department managers describe problems of getting the right staff and lacking the power of participating in such decisions. The extra clerical employees required at the health records and information department could only be expected to come from the executive office or the headquarters. This leads to resignation of the staff, who feel that there are no solutions for the problems encountered such as the need for extra manpower to assist in clerical tasks. This can be understood as an indication that the decisions in the sector do not reflect the observed realities at work. Consider also that there was a complaint that the

HMIS department was headed by "people from the wrong profession". Medical doctors heading such departments are a manifestation that staffing is not guided by approaches of getting the right people who qualify for the tasks necessary; such decisions are done with no regard to the real needs.

Essence of reporting

Probably a more distinguishing observation is the one directly related to the preparation and submission of reports in the sector. Reporting is understood as being answerable to the higher cadres, managers and supervisors. Incidences show that the facility department is expecting the reform of tools to come from the headquarters. They are not in a position to contribute in the correction of tools and are left helpless using tools and formats that do not fit the actual realities they encounter in reporting. They are not expected to adapt the reports to be relevant since the headquarters is not ready to relax requirements on expected reporting formats. Called upon to participate in reviewing the tools, the staffs misunderstood the initiative as an attempt to increase their workloads or to expose problems in their processes. They can only identify with reporting projects having been about introduction of computers and meetings being about sitting back and taking notes on what are to be done next. Invitation to contribution in a meeting is understood as pinpointing a problem in one's department. This limits the possibilities of making from-within changes that reflect the actual needs. The changes are coming from outside the staff's scope of operation.

Feedback from reporting obligations

The influence of the prevailing organizational structure to reporting is further seen in terms of feedback from the reports prepared. There is no corresponding feedback in the reporting cycle. The facility staff sends the reports but do not get any feedback, neither do they see a reflection of their reports' contents in the planning. There seems to be an endorsement from lower cadres. The incident of the ministry official who was using his seven years old report as the most current report depicts this. Responses that depict doubts of whether a staff's contribution will count, whether recommendations will be followed or in the worst case scenario, it will work to his/her disadvantage, depict sanctioning by the lower cadres to the situation of having limited feedback channels in the reporting processes.

5.2. Non participative nature of work with limited empowerment and democracy at workplace

Activities that call for collaborative working, requiring input from the various representations in a team are only successful if they are done with a participative approach. Participation is however dependent on having empowered team members who freely contribute to the discussions and make inputs in an effort to unfold realities of the situation they find themselves in (at the work place) and co-construct the solutions that address the real situations at work. By co-construction of solutions I mean the participants are able to find solutions as a group in processes that as individuals they would not be able to arrive at. From the case story described, there are various incidences that indicate prevalence of a non-participative culture that limits the extent to which staff are empowered to make contributions in decisions that influence their work lives. Some of these incidences include:

Culture of silence and "reactionary working"

The reporting process is initiated from the top management and is characterized by uncertainty of the lower cadre staff of what is likely to be requested and with what urgency. That translates to more hours of work for those preparing the report. The missed opportunities for reflection from the 'foot soldiers' of the sector, as curtailed by a reactionary attitude of waiting for reports to be requested, is a manifestation of lack of empowerment for the lower cadre staff in the sector. Work practices have degenerated to routines. The opposite would be active, energetic and proactive presentation of reports and enthusiastic contribution in meetings. On the contrary, the observed is silence in meetings, poor freedom of expression as depicted by staff not willing to describe what they do but listen to what they are supposed to do. In a workplace featuring democratic values, freedom of expression, participation and contribution to the actual realities of the work process would not be at one's own risk, and it would be clear how experiences matter. As demonstrated by the incidence of handing over the whole processes of reporting morbidity and mortality, an empowered work environment is not promoted. Such would be manifested by clarity of the importance of their experiences over time, meaning they have a place in the computer supported processes.

Innovation and improvement expectations

The assistance of the developed prototype enabling the timely submission of the morbidity and mortality report from "Hillside" was received with surprise. It was not expected that a helpful initiative can come from below in the hierarchy. Moreover, from the experiences in the lower levels, the proposition to adapt the list of diseases used by medical personnel at those regions was received as an insult. It was not expected that the staff collecting data and preparing reports would not only be partners in making changes to tools but also be the providers of the knowledge that forms the point of departure for the changes. Further, this issue is demonstrated by the problem of one group presenting what they expect to be happening and the other not admitting the actual realities of how the work gets done. Only a moderated formulation of anticipated processes was a compromise of the two presentations. This demonstrated that participative contributions from members of a team needed to be moderated as opposed to the free flowing contributions that would be characteristic of a workplace characterized by empowerment and democratic space.

Inclusiveness decision making

Looking back, the fact that the headquarters granted the research permit without a requirement to get an introduction from the district/facility, also shows how work arrangement and responsibilities are not democratically understood. It would have been expected that a research permit is to be granted if the facility is identifying with it and therefore needs an introduction.

5.3. Non existence of an information culture depicted by weak support for communication

Whereas information technologies (and associated tools like computers) constitute the landscape of modern day organizations such as the health sector, the personal attitudes and perspectives towards information makes the difference in determining whether the tools are useful or not. By information culture I mean that what influences the value with which information is taken in the context of work. It is also about how the information artifacts are treated in an organization, the unwritten unconscious behavior that fills the gap between what officially is said to happen and what really happens irrespective of the ICT tools. It touches on the channels and the attitudes enabling forwarding of information to make it useful by being at the right place at the right time.

Below I describe my observations that point towards behavior and values that influence information use. Some of these incidences from the described cases include:

Awareness of linkages in tasks and responsibilities
A meeting bringing together the hospital departments to discuss the information processes with the intention of unfolding information channels and accompanying processes. It emerged that several departments did not understand the information activities going on in another department. Such comments as *"the records people don't understand our work yet they want us to report"* depict a situation of missing links in understanding the role of information that is at the heart of collaborative work amongst the hospital staff. It also emerged that the staffs do not have information at their finger tips. Consider for example how requests from headquarters put pressure on the staff at the hospital in preparing requested reports. The realization of what can be reported is first understood when the request arrives. Also the fact that reports submitted are not processed to manageable formats for providing answers without making urgent requests to the facilities is another example of the same issue experienced at the headquarters.

Information use
I understand the observation of failed feedback processes as coming from an underlying attitude to information. The value of information would be expected to be reflected in subsequent plans – especially from headquarters. For example, staff postings and allocations were said not to be reflective of the information reported in earlier reports. The non - follow-up after submitting reports and the failure to see if the sector use of information at the source is another incident.

Dedicated IT department
All in all, the non - existence of an IT department in the sector from the headquarters down to the public hospital is a reflection of the perspectives with which information is appreciated. The department that takes up the role, HMIS then happens to be required to produce a report every three years. This coming from a sector whose information lifespan can be said to be very short indicates the non - prevalence of an information culture. The recognition and description of the records department as the hospital's "IT department" can be attributed to the vibrancy of its activities that are given more weight by the recognized relevance of its reports contents. This recognition is a pointer to a developing information culture that needs nurturing.

5.4. Constrained opportunities for learning and technical exposure

Another observed issue relates to constraints in terms of opportunities for learning and further professional (capacity) development. By capacity development opportunities I mean access to processes by which individuals are able to enhance their skills and abilities required to identify and understand challenges in their daily work activities meant to achieve their objectives. CIDA (2000) defines capacity development as *"the approaches, strategies and methodologies used by developing country, and/or external stakeholders, to improve performance at the individual, organizational, network/sector or broader system level."*

Capacity development schemes

From my experiences, I observed that the staff, especially those at the health records and information department who can be considered the information specialists, did not have opportunities to upgrade their skills as did their medical officers counterparts. Deliberately or unknowingly there are no systematic skill upgrading opportunities for the staff. The opportunities for seminars, workshops and other forums are abused given the financial benefits they bring (in terms of allowances). The seminars and workshops end up being attended by superiors irrespective of their lines of duty.

From the interactions with the Ministry of Health's officers, it became clear that the assumption that the officers were exposed to technology developments in the areas relevant to their work was wrong. With constrained staff in the ministry, pressures from daily routines and the lack of internet connectivity translated to limited opportunities for keeping abreast with technological developments. Discussions revolving around decisions on technologies to use in the project had to include assistance in setting up the development environments. This constrained thorough evaluation of technologies that comes with hands - on experience.

5.5. Methodical responses in response to the issues

Faced with the realities of the issues described above, in subsequent project interactions, there are specific ways in which I responded to ensure the project establishment went on. In this section I highlight how I handled prevalence of the issues in the context as experienced in the case stories. These are the basis of the detailed reflection that informs the propositions for methodological approaches that I present in the next chapter.

5.5.1. Appreciation of informal consultations

Being aware of the power influences in dealing with the health sector players, to achieve results one needs to target the right level of influence. As argued elsewhere in this report, the power reality must be the point of departure in attempts to engage in a process aimed at transforming that reality. In the second phase of my experiences in the sector while working with the donor agency, the concept of informal consultations has played a great role.

Top management consultations
The communication channels used in the project engagements are very diverse with the written communications (e.g. emails) representing advanced discussions where decisions have already been made. This mode of communication is clear from emails inviting prospective project team members for initial meetings. The lobbying that is necessary with the stakeholders wielding power is done preliminary to formal invitations in various forums such other regular meetings and activities of their work. The HDWG consultations that preceded the initial engagement is a good reflection of this. The chair of the group, the management of the ministry's departments and potential agencies with the resources for the initiative, made their commitments informally prior to this. This is reproduced in project 3 where the decisions on the project process had been made informally prior to the workshop session.

Set up of "reference groups"
For projects representing stakeholders from across several organizations, the challenge of participative engagement is managing the group of possible participants. The *modus operandi* adopted in my experiences is one of having smaller reference groups from the large health donor working group (project 2) as well as from the different organizations that were represented in the technical working group (project 3). The selection of the reference group was done on the basis of the existing relationships in the groups. Although voluntary participation in the reference groups was the criteria for membership, it is clear that the capabilities of the organizations influenced the memberships. There is internal undocumented knowledge amongst the sector players that guided the processes. This internal knowledge of each other is a crucial pointer to a mechanism for defusing power relations. Reference groups in the projects ensured that it was easier and manageable to have consultations amongst the members for consensus building (even on ad hoc ways).

5.5.2. Identification of specific focus in interactions

A major problem with strict power relations is the helplessness that less powerful members of a group undergo in decisions touching on their areas of work. Such are the realities experienced in terms of limitations in empowerment and undemocratic workplace arrangements. Such a scenario presents a non - participative nature of work. The adopted strategy in response to these realities is one of consciously being aware of the competencies and specializations that must be brought forth for the success of the project establishment exercise. An example is the need to understand how a document gets generated and published in the sector. Whereas the specialists directly involved in the process may be less empowered in decisions as to whether the workflow should be made collaboratively with other organizations and how, it's important that as a project manager one characterizes the issues raised in terms of the competency fields of the people participating in the workflow. Through the characterization into technical, professional and managerial aspects, eases the negative aspects of un-participative or poor empowerment. This in my experiences necessitated deferring discussion to future visits/consultations with specific participants. See for example the need for collaboration with thematic groups of the HDWG in project 2. In project 3, the various organizations as per religious affiliations (protestant, catholic, Muslim) were engaged individually through their IT representatives.

5.5.3. Coaching and lobbying initiatives

Working in a team where some members are technologically disadvantaged in comparison with others, the capability for collaboration can differ in the team. One cause of differences in capabilities is the differences in getting opportunities to learn about technological developments. The constraints under which work gets done in developing countries' government institutions contribute to degraded levels of information for professional developments. For example, whereas opportunities for internet search are readily available in the developed countries, this is not the case in developing countries. This means there should be no assumptions about the differences in levels of knowledge about new technologies amongst technology experts from these two contexts. The challenge from this is to engage processes that will coach the project team members to creatively achieve more with the realities of their work situations. Through this, I tapped into the willingness and preparedness to learn in the sector to the extent that my project partners made great progress. A concrete engagement process is the allocation of tasks to research on and the responsible person report in subsequent meetings. I provided initial links as a basis for further links and presentations were very encouraging. Moreover, aware that a section of the team is having difficulties that would play negatively in a next meeting I adopted "preparatory meetings" with the team members. This is related to the promotion of interaction moments but goes further to have aspects of lobbying for more motivation on the part of the team for the tasks at hand.

6. Facilitating Resonance in Project Establishment
6.1. The premise
Developing countries present unique contexts characterized by issues that profoundly influence and render PD practice different from Western contexts. I have in the preceding chapters argued around the major issue of intense power relations and identified from my empirical experiences issues that set the developing countries context different. Some of the issues I have identified in the previous chapters include:
- A culture of intensive power relations supported by the organization structure,
- Non - participative nature of work with limited empowerment and democracy at the workplace
- Non - existence of an information culture depicted by weak support for communication
- Constrained opportunities for learning, for technical exposure and for continued professional development

These issues confront project establishment efforts in the contexts. They are especially relevant in participatory approaches that seek to bring together the users (with consideration of existing workplace realities) and technology proponents (designers and project sponsors). Moreover, when emphasis in a project process is shifted from mere technical concerns to organizational concerns, the very success or failure of the project revolves around how these issues are addressed.

In recognition of the issues' static and entrenched nature in the context, it would be naive to seek their dismantling or eradication in a revolutionary change process within a project setting. Projects are transitory and short-lived in comparison to organizational structures that are static and long-lived. In this state of affairs, the process of successfully establishing projects needs to have a clear and specific focus on methods that seek to address the issues and tame the context's limiting factors within the project's constraints of time, productivity and quality. In the long run the proposed approach is a focus meant to influence the organizational culture (its perception and practice) and to defuse power intensity by creatively providing moments during which participants become unaware of the power they do (or do not) wield, ultimately bringing about re-orientations of perspectives with regard to embracing IS technologies. The process recognizes the need for flexibility in the context – driven by contextual issues especially to accommodate changes in the context as well as knowledge and attitudes of the project stakeholders.

6.2. Model Adaptation – First experiences

6.2.1. The use of JAD in STEPS

As described in this study, I faced challenges settling in the sector since I had to integrate myself into the "way the ministry works". I was initially bogged down by administrative issues that resulted in slow progress before any observable progress in the project. There was no indication of participatory ideals taking root in the form of collaboration in a group. Whereas the interviews, observations and other interactions were very informative and I was getting to understand the reality of work in the sector, it was clear from my background in software development that I needed an explicit methodology as a tool to arrive at agreed upon initial requirements that could be implemented. For this I needed a methodology founded in leveraging group dynamics. Based on this, I adopted Joint Application Development (JAD)'s explicitly defined phases (Wood & Silver 1995) that lead to the generation of an agreed - upon document. summarizes the 5 phases of JAD. Moreover, JAD was appealing because it accommodates group dynamics in a process that consolidates individual, small groups and large groups' interaction results.

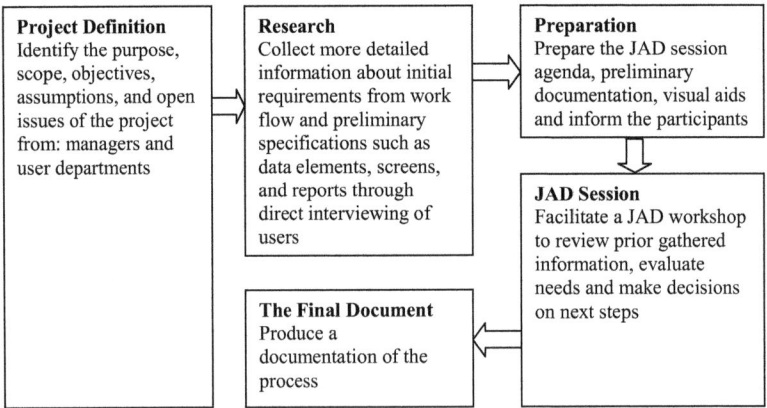

Figure 28: JAD Steps (adapted from Chung et al. 2006)

Through following of JAD, I benefited from a controlled process backed by tangible deliverables that imposed discipline amongst project partners. From an initial motivation to just bring together project partners to "talk it out", the JAD process enabled joint production of an initial model in the form of a workflow that the stakeholders agreed upon. From this jointly produced model I was able to develop an initial prototype that fit directly to the hospital process. In the context of the power relations, the JAD process was instrumental in initiating collaboration and joint meeting of three layers in the organization structure of the ministry: the facility, the district and the provincial health administration levels. This contributed to mutual understanding of the project through the invitation of participants to share their insights and perspectives amongst themselves.

I adopted the view that JAD as a process can be applied to fill activities for a methodical approach in executing the STEPS model. I executed a series of JAD processes to achieve STEPS's project initiation step as follows: The preparation of the project proposal and the detailed information I shared with the hospital and other ministry staff clarifying the objectives and visions of the project served as the JAD's phase 1. This established the stakeholders' views on the project and I aimed at securing their support of the idea. Moreover, I sought to identify the key departments and corresponding staffs who were to form the key close collaborators in the project. This was followed by further discussions and meetings with the stakeholders to identify the work realities in the hospital. E.g. the processes involved in one department's reporting obligations were thoroughly documented (phase 2 of JAD). I held sessions that brought together various groups of stakeholders: departmental, cross departmental and district health management team. The preparation involved inviting the key resource persons, preparing the agenda and other logistics for the meeting (phase 3 of JAD). The workshops and other group meetings formed the session described by JAD's phase 4. The last phase was realized through production of short briefing notes from the meetings and workshop proceedings shared with the stakeholders.

By following similar approach in later projects in which I bring the two methodologies together within a framework of participation and collaboration, I have managed to elicit initial project functional requirements in a joint setting in ways that are responsive to work place realities. Once there is a favorable reception and the project activities are seen to progress in manageable time spans, consolidation of the project process follows with the users taking control as per the STEPS model.

6.2.2. Proposition of using JAD & STEPS for project establishment

I summarize the incorporation of JAD when doing project establishment in terms of the following iterative sequence of action steps:

- Preparation of a summary of the project objectives in the spirit of JAD's phase 1. The goal is to communicate the project idea to the extent that any differences in the conceptual formulation of the need for the project are clarified. Contentious issues are brought forth and a clear representation of the contentious (open) issues is made. An initial draft of the scope is established and ready to be refined. Draft here signifies that the document is not required to be comprehensive and it must be prepared in a way that the contentious issues are clearly stated as being open for discussion.

- Joint analysis of the processes that are targets of the project with the actual executors of those processes. The objective is to establish the reality in which the work gets done via sustained and detailed interactions. To successfully achieve this, IT experts need to have gained some knowledge of those target processes and they should be anticipative to propose relevant technological solutions to address concerns from the stakeholders. It is important that the selection of the participants in the discussions should reflect the realities of the organization (e.g. not be limited to a single level of only managers/supervisors). The intra-group conflicts expose scenarios upon which a foundation for consensus can be initiated through structured negotiations. Negotiations structured as exchanges that promote the learning advocated by STEPS.

- Formal selection of a project group tasked to spearhead the project. This specifically involves the identification of group members who become a core project team mandated to drive the process right from preparation of initial meeting agendas (c.f STEPS' baselines). STEPS also advocates selection of a project team during project initiation.

- Holding at least one joint meeting of the project stakeholders to discuss the project ideas and conflicts captured in earlier interactions. Whereas a single meeting with diverse representations might serve to commission the project, it is the case that several meetings will be necessary as I noticed in my experiences. A technique to bring the contentious issues in the sessions is to use confrontation as discussed in (Bardram 2000, Floyd et al 1989b p. 311).

- Sharing of the deliberations from the meetings, highlighting where consensus has been achieved and the open issues. In the spirit of STEPS baselines, it's important to include group action points, as next steps which signify an ongoing process.

6.2.3. Evaluation of this approach

There are several gains of this approach such as facilitating establishment of a working team relationship among the system developers and the key players, facilitating elicitation of implicit information as inroads to a new domain, laying grounds for sustained documentation, establishment of a common vocabulary which simplifies review of project deliverables (Anderson 1994). However, this approach fails to address salient social issues of a context (e.g. empowerment problems), puts a lot of pressure on designers by requiring that they be experts in facilitation and is likely to fall into the problem of sanctioning existing organizational imbalances (e.g. when stereotypes in the organization become the key informants). Moreover, it needs a good command of confidence in the technical experts by the stakeholders. In my assessment, as argued by Jones (1997), JAD seeks to build group consensus orientation in an undemocratic and technically oriented audience. From my experiences in the sector I have found it handy in mitigating "problems of entry" (to initiate the project process) as a prelude to more thorough application of participatory design ideas. An entry to the context requires demonstration of competence and early technical functionalities that go a long way in building confidence and motivation for sustained participation.

6.3. A new orientation

6.3.1. Pointer to major issues in the context

Whereas I was successful in establishing my first project in the sector and developed a prototype, my engagement was interrupted and the project did not progress beyond the prototype. At this point, my research goal to enrich the STEPS model by applying it in a new context was far from being realized. Upon reflection I was able to situate my experiences in a wider perspective as relates to practice of PD in specific contexts. As discussed in (Kiura 2006) my reflection is summarized as recognition of the fact that information systems are implemented in existing organizational landscapes and to find ways through these landscapes, it is important for the adopted process to have a closer orientation to prevalent social realities. These landscapes are shaped by established ways of working that are deeply inscribed into the organization forming a defined culture. As a result of the reflection my later project establishment work in the sector has been closely influenced by an awareness of the existence of a national culture and my approach adapted to be sensitive to the realities of empowerment, democracy and freedom of expression in the sector. I took the perspective that contextual realities provide a foundation of successful project establishment if a facilitating process is engaged that supports translation of the culture to be favorable for project establishment. The organizational realities confronting my adaptation of STEPS were brining to the foreground fundamental PD ideals upon which STEPS is based but which are only implicitly referred to in its description.

Information systems introduction following a participation informed model like STEPS requires collaboration between various groups of people in a setting characterized by negotiating changes that the introduced system is bound to bring about. A study attributed to the research community behind STEPS describes collaboration in projects as being about carrying out joint activities in ways that promote creation of joint experiences that lead to *"development of a common basis of competence"* between the users and designers (Floyd et al. 1989b, p. 310). In the limited time that is available to establish a project, the level to which a "common basis of competence" can be achieved is limited. What I propose is that the communication support of the applied methodologies needs to promote alignment of the project stakeholders to each other's activities, responsibilities, know-how and to contextual realities that are experienced. The thrust of this proposition is the call to systematically establish a situation whereby collaboration efforts are geared towards support for understanding each other with respect to a common goal of the project. The underlying reasons for issues observed in a context can then be elicited, captured and presented so that a process to overcome them is engaged. Such a process will connect with work realities in a context by showing empathy, providing inspiration to address tacit aspects and promoting engagement. In the spirit of PD, this recognizes that the solution to address experienced contextual problems lies with all the project stakeholders. The goal is to collaboratively construct the problem by bridging the gaps manifested in the project team. In a project establishment undertaking there are two major gaps that are encountered. First is the gap represented by difference in domains expertise (users versus designers). Secondly there is the gap that exists between the methods and the application context. The challenge that arises is therefore one of trying to bridge these gaps. By promoting communication, gaps that cause conflicts in project establishment can be addressed. This calls for an explanation of a view of communication that promotes the essence of collaboration in PD.

6.3.2. Resonance metaphor for PD communication

The widely adopted and used communication theory is based on the conduit metaphor (St. Clair 1999). Communication is understood as involving transmission of information by putting messages into established forms (patterns, symbols, letters, etc) and then sending these messages through channels (the conduit) to the receiver who retrieves the messages. Whereas based on this theory it is possible to articulate complex phenomena and by channeling messages to others share our knowledge, this understanding has been criticized for failing to place more emphasis on how communication supports the establishment of common knowledge. Creation of common knowledge is the essence of communication as depicted by the original word used for communication in Latin *communicare* whose literal translation is "to make common" (cf. Cortes & Carlos 1997, p. 578). This essence of communication is very essential in endeavors seeking to initiate participatory practice. According to Huesca (1995, p. 101) *"one reason that participatory models of practice have eluded scholars is that, by and large, researchers have ignored the communicative procedures by which participation is implemented in everyday life"*. Literature from Latin America, philosophically grounded in the writings of Freire (1970, 1973) champions the critique of this dominant theory of communication. For example Beltrán (1975, 1980)'s "horizontal communication" model is based on access, participation, dialogue, grassroots involvement and promotion of democracy. This alternative model demonstrated the differences between the Western and non-Western cultures when dealing with accommodation of other cultural aspects when pursuing a valued goal, such as in a development program. A major criticism is based on the observation that this theory of communication does no promote the alignment of activities to the realities in the non-Western cultures. For example Beltrán concluded that *"the classic diffusion model was based on an ideological framework that contradicts the reality of this region"* (Beltrán 1975, p.190 as used in Huesca 2003).

I take from this orientation that communication in PD processes should serve to promote the alignment of interactions to the daily struggles of a community in a given context. In the daily realities of a context are intra-context conflicts that are to be tamed to build a foundation for a contextually relevant solution based on involvement. A dialogical approach, such as suggested by Winschiers (2003) in carrying out technology transfer projects in developing countries can be understood as one promoting this alternative view of communication in PD practice. The objective is to incorporate local views, voices and perspectives in non-Western contexts by synthesizing experiences and know-how so that project stakeholders are able to identify with the wisdom of others and hence that of the context. This is analogous to the achievement of resonance in the project amongst the project stakeholders. In much the same way that, when struck, a tuning fork emits vibrations that are picked by other forks sharing the same frequency to a melodious output, communication in PD needs to be one that promotes the resonance of the people involved. In the physical world, resonance (or colloquially sympathetic vibration) is the way to get maximum transfer of energy (Elfrey 2000) while in the social world communication resonance is the way to get a maximum transfer of a message's content. Communication is to establish a state of resonance between two persons where a receiver of a message resonates with the contents and reinforces the communication (Gärdenfors 1996). In a state of resonating communication, the messages exchanged are "in tune" and the responses amplify the contents. In a PD approach, such an orientation of a methodology can serve to ensure reflecting with others, not for them, hence dissolving many of the tensions encountered in IS projects in non - Western contexts. Project establishment is therefore about setting up processes to induce resonance.

An information system will lead to changes in an organization and therefore the process of establishing a project should brace itself to be confronted by resistance as the current organizational realities get challenged. Conflicts in the realities of work are inevitable as new ways of working and work organization are seen to confront organization realities (such the organization structure) that are sanctioned by the status quo. In this case, in the spirit of trying to establish resonance, it is important to build capacity for negotiation, where conflicts involving different views and sometimes contrasting convictions can be voiced and argued out with the aim to overcome them in an atmosphere of mutual respect driven by an overriding motivation to cooperate. These are aspects prominent in the Scandinavian approach that seeks to achieve humanization and democracy by putting into consideration issues of job satisfaction, workplace design and safety in the design of information systems (Floyd et al. 1989b). My concentration on communication stipulates that project development proceeds on the assumption of a project specific consensus, enabling all those involved being motivated to collaborate on a common mission. In the face of conflicting interests, values and perspectives the goal is to find consensus by way of conflict resolution approaches. This line of thought is inspired by the collective resource approach whose motivation is on how *"computer technology should be applied in the interests of the working population"* (Floyd et. al 1989b, p. 268).

The working population is to be understood as the whole organizational context that is in some way affected by the information system under development (cf. my argument for a holistic view in PD as opposed to in shop floor level only in -chapter 4). With this understanding, in a PD process communication is meant to help "constitute social structures" where properties of individuals are aligned and relations are constituted in the context of a (project) activity (Allwood 1995). Communication will serve to coordinate social activities not only internally between persons that engage in an activity but also externally are engaged seen as cooperation between an activity such as project establishment and people external to the activity in the organization or organizational units.

6.4. *Resonance facilitators in PD methodological approaches*

By incorporating and pursuing this resonance seeking communication, existing methodological approaches for project establishment can be enriched to overcome disconnection with context-specific issues and exploit the wisdom. The goal is to seek consensus of ideas and mutual understanding that is sustained by empowerment of the project stakeholders in a continued learning process that makes available the realities of the context for change by embracing new working realities. I propose that project establishment approaches should enrich their focus to include the following:

- Aligning to what is familiar
- Embracing a coaching orientation
- Dedicating ample time
- Using shared visualizations

These are discussed next in more detail with an aim to explain the underlying principles to propose how they can be achieved to especially promote defusing of intense power relations through seeking of resonance amongst project stakeholders.

6.4.1. Aligning to what is familiar (for bonding)

Objectives:
- Establish bonding with the context realities using *development from within* methods
- Build a relationship depicting integration and devoid of hostile references to "them" versus "us" in the interactions

In the pursuit of trying to establish resonance amongst the project stakeholders, a first objective in project establishment is to seek alignment to the realities of the context. The tools and methods adopted to initiate the engagement need to identify with what the project stakeholders are familiar with. This follows from the concept of development-from-within seeking to tap into existing competencies and promoting feeling of continuity, involvement and gradual change from the present contextual reality. Gradually the users identify their experiences as the point of departure for the re-arrangements of workplace structures that will be occasioned by the project results. The objective is to promote bonding (establishment of relationships) to the extent that project participants, irrespective of areas of expertise, positions, responsibilities, attitudes and interests feel to be sharing a common fate: the success of the project. Strong bonding is achievable through appraisal of endogenous realities of the context as seen in present and past locally experienced initiatives. Through identity with what project stakeholders experience in the context, project establishment benefits from enriched contributions, active engagement and articulation above the haze of complex work processes.

Methods:

- Doing a detailed stakeholder identification and analysis to expose the values, perspectives, resources and organizational norms associated with the context. This should include identification and representation of existing relationships upon which the context draws its identity and which thereby influence how work is done.
- Identifying the competencies in place as pointers to strategies that work in the context. This should include how power relations are coped with, what partnerships exist and what are their influences.
- Role playing through participation in the daily activities of the organization to open up more insights in the realities of the context's complexity beyond the general assumptions and descriptions of the activities.

The competencies required for this step include the ability to learn rapidly and progressively in the context settings; the ability to balance experienced reality with assumptions (methodological biases); the ability to adapt to the context challenges of poor or no infrastructure, limited resources, language barriers, etc; the ability to use extensive triangulation of the methods used to build intimacy with the context; ability to demonstrate empowering of the stakeholders by sharing responsibility especially in tasks touching on context aspectsthat are likely to change; etc.

This step has a very ambitious objective of integration into (in most cases) unknown contexts. The techniques I propose to achieve this emanate from the concepts of phatic communication as the means by which social channels are opened. Casalegno & McWilliam (2004) describe phatic communication as exchanges made up of ready-made sentences or common and expected statements meant to establish a contact without transmitting any precise content because what is important is not the "content" but the fact that the exchange takes place. An attempt should be made to be aware of and practice the relational rituals of the context with regard to formalism, modes of expression and any other behavioral codes. The content of interactions should in this case take a second priority by adopting a role reversal whereby technical experts become the "learners" and the stakeholders become "teachers" providing the "learners" with expert knowledge of the complexities of the local conditions (Chambers 1994). Beyond what people in a culture of silence write down (or formally describe), non-formal (sometimes verbal) communication can lead to identification of emotions, attitudes and perspectives in the context. These are the "bonding points" for establishing resonance with them as they relate directly to the underlying factors that influence the observed features in the context.

Through reduction of interaction distances via bonding, mutual understanding is built as foundation upon which distribution, sharing and diffusion of knowledge takes place.

6.4.2. Embracing a coaching orientation

Objective:
- Adopt coaching-oriented methods that promote preparedness and freedom of expression (articulation)

To exploit the benefits of the bonding achieved above, the focus turns to ensure sustained interaction. The interactions are designed to maintain a high-level view of the project objectives while being closely associated with the solution of immediate problems. This is achieved by interactions demonstrating a fit to the context by their support of capabilities exercised to achieve daily tasks. The users are at liberty to critique their processes and "dream" about technological and work re-organization solutions. Technical experts on the other hand establish rapport that allows them to assimilate the organizational context issues and share their observations with the users. In the ensuing exchange, the project team members are coached to expand their views about their work and technical know-how especially as concerns available technical solutions. Individual convictions, attitudes and beliefs are exposed upon which a self-evaluation and critique process develops. Through this the users unlock their potential thereby expanding their views about their work. Individual convictions and beliefs especially for those not wielding much power are entertained through clear demonstration of how their roles and experiences are indispensable inputs to any future solution.

The aim is to engage interactions through which the stakeholders get into dialogue with their own context in the same way a coachee unlocks own potential to achieve more results that exceed normal results without a coach. I draw this concept of coaching as applied to executive coaching as *"a helping relationship formed between a client.....and a consultant who uses a wide variety of behavioral techniques and methods ... to achieve a mutually identified set of goals ..."* (Kilburg 1996 cited in Peel 2005, p. 19). This description highlights that the process takes the form of establishing a mutual relationship that sets a goal to be achieved by the users. The mutual setting of the goal drives the process with a conscious effort to keep the users as the focus in the process. Through these interactions, context -specific issues will be confronted. A prominent issue that works contra participation is the limited freedom of expression. By creatively engaging individual and informal discussion sessions that seek user convenience, such contra -participation aspects of the context can be adjourned. Adjourned to refer to situations in which one will become expressive as s/he engages in a discussion touching on his her line of responsibility without much reference to external hierarchical relations.

Methods
- Having interviews in informal sessions not only at the individual level but also in controlled groups. Such groups include "project reference groups" and cross - departmental groups whose definition is beyond the project establishment exercise.
- Having regular meetings ("stammtisch") sessions designed to report and review observations. In these sessions it is sought to have analysis provoking evaluation of situations that the users take for granted as daily routines.

The requirement for this step is the ability to build trust, confidentiality and communication within a partnership; ability to incorporate multi-level active engagements characterized by listening skills; the ability to generate powerful questions that lead to expanding views towards a future vision. The goal of the exercise in this case develops to one of assisting people delve into thinking beyond their routine practices. The previous alignment to context now becomes a stepping stone on which anticipated future settings are visualized. Through the sustained interaction and promotion of freedom of expression, a meaning of the present is constructed and since the future is embedded in the present by way of projections, anticipations, hopes and desires (cf. St. Clair 2007) it follows that new contextual re-organization designs as consequences of the project will be identified.

6.4.3. Dedicating ample time (to witness learning)

Objective:
- Promoting learning through conducive settings that allow for reflection and participation

Having adopted a coaching perspective in the interactions and letting the stakeholders drive the initiative with self-reflection to achieve own mutually set goals, it is necessary to promote learning that is necessary to deal with future changes. The objective is to include all perspectives in the project process regardless of the organizational status of those with divergent perspectives.

Following up on the analogy of resonance in communication, it is important to note that others resonate with our messages by having a capacity to interpret those messages (cf. resonance associated with messages of love to people with related experiences). In physical resonance this capacity is comparable to the existence of an internal frequency that is necessary in resonating objects. On this perspective, a listener is no longer a passive "receiver" of a ready-packed message, but is actively taking part in creating the information and the associated meaning. Through a learning process that integrates negotiation and dialogue, a condition for mutual capacity is created. Promoting learning serves to contribute to resolving conflicts between different perspectives. As illustrated in my experience, this is however inhibited by organizational and structural realities in the context that discourage being outspoken or even acknowledging experience. Incorporation of multiple perspectives and ability to build a compromise on future scenarios of work is curtailed when people do not speak unless spoken to or asked a question. Reflections and a capacity to learn are inhibited when people are uncomfortable being called upon to speak and not to just note down what to do next (Kiura 2006). Explicit awareness and embrace of methods for empowering such silent participants to engage in discussions about decisions made by those perceived to have power will promote the interpretation support necessary for resonance. For example integrating the brainstorming principle of "all input counts" in interaction-moments (chapter 4) can serve to stimulate reflection and provide first opportunities for active engagement. This is essential in the political process of negotiating allocation of resources and prioritizing goals during project establishment.

Methods
- Distribute responsibilities amongst the stakeholders based on competencies or according to rules previously agreed upon. In my experiences, I found that assigning a lower cadre staff a time slot to present in a workshop and moderate questions from his/her

presentation was very helpful. 'Assignments' to a team member to research on an aspect of the project (e.g. possible technology platforms for the project) opened up reflection and engagement with opportunities for learning across the project team.
- Change environments. People's behavior is influenced by environments in which they are in, demonstrated by unconsciously following specific patterns when in certain surroundings. Moreover, it is important to avoid the disorientation and distraction that comes from work surroundings. For example at the workplace surroundings it was unimaginable for some one-to-one exchanges to take place but while in workshops outside the work place in relaxed settings, one-to-one exchanges (including critique) ensued.
- Provide ample time for reflection, patiently offering opportunities for absorption, interpretation and response. The goal is to have a setting in which the users (and designers alike) are freed from feelings of rushed understanding of what is presented, reaching an informed decision and being required to respond.

6.4.4. Using shared visualizations (based on moderation)

Objective:
- Production of a group-generated and mutually agreed representation

Project establishment is shown by production of a common way forward (cf. baselines in STEPS). It is necessary that irrespective of the context features inhibiting PD, contributions from the interactions are ably reconciled. The situation of intensive power imbalances, democratically challenged workplace settings and limited opportunities for skill advancement introduces challenges for any approach meant to achieve this. The objective is to produce tangible manifestations of the engagements that not only depict consensus but have been subjected to a process leading to mutual agreement. An artifact arrived at this way is a production of all the project stakeholders. The artifact is meant to capture real results of the engagements in a concrete form just as a scenario in scenario-based design (Boedker 2000) is a concrete story about the people, tasks and assumptions in the observed environment. Taking the different submissions (viewpoints) as scenarios, this step proposes a shared representation (e.g. graphically when in a group setting). Differing views and perspectives are captured from a group as they extend and critique a shared visualization. My proposed technique is to iteratively generate the artifact in a way that captures assumptions and encourages reflection through revision, extensions and/or reductions. The artifact generation process starts with the most fundamental version that opens up the group and dilutes manifestations of strict power relations as either more details are added to accommodate other perspectives or fewer details are adopted to remove ambiguity and contradictions. This way it is possible to initiate and sustain active contribution and feedback processes through which the representation evolves to be a creation of the whole group.

Methods:
This proposition follows from methods that emphasize interaction such as use of mock-ups, prototypes and iterative design. However, I stress the support for active contributions and visualization. In the process, several versions of an artifact are generated from a process characterized by presenting different perspectives, setting the problem, identifying alternative solutions, negotiating an agreed course of action (consensus) and identifying potential problems. Through moderation the versions are developed further with the use of such techniques as consensus seeking time off, distributed breaks, drills that stage a walkthrough of visualized processes, etc. Search for resonance is manifested in instances when the discussion is allowed to focus on a specific interaction-moment guided by a contentious issue about which consensus is needed.

Why visualization?
I argue that visualization plays a very important role in the building of conditions for resonance. Visualization serves as a means to reveal and share what Gärdenfors (2004) refers to as "inner worlds". He defines an inner world as *"the collection of all detached representations ... and their interrelations"*. By detached representation he refers to conceptualization of objects that are not present in current situations, "things that are not perceptually present" (ibid, p. 238-239). During project establishment, the future organizational realities to be achieved through the project exist as visions not currently present in the organization, though derived from current situations. Through visualization, project team members bring out and share with each other their conceptualizations (visions) as regards the project process and the goals. Communicating about these *"individual models of the future"* and refining them iteratively leads to a consensually

agreed - upon version that forms the basis for team members to resonate with each other's views and perspectives. Cooperation in project establishment is therefore to be seen as founded in the ability to represent, access and communicate detached representations in much the same way multi-perspective approaches call for conscious *"elaborating, contrasting and combining views of the same area of interest from different angles in order to gain deeper insights"* (Floyd et al. 1989b, p. 315). By sharing visualizations, achievement of resonance amongst the project stakeholders is facilitated.

6.5. Implications

6.5.1. Concrete implications to project establishment results

The four resonance facilitators I have proposed above have implications that relate to the practice of information systems design, development and deployment as an intervention in reality. This means they facilitate a process that leads to changes in the context. In the process, basic methods are contextualized to address context - specific issues. I present an argument that from embracing the concepts behind my propositions, there are concrete changes in the context and eventually in the results of the establishment process.

My study has taken the case of projects involving several organizations (or organization units) with representatives from these organizations forming the membership of project teams. I recognize that a project establishment exercise involves several activities and processes. As a process I summarize the exercise as one progressing from identifying a need (and generation of an idea), analysis of the need (involving communication of the idea, inventory of status quo – processes and people), composing a project team that sets the scope of the project, getting a commitment for the project (resources, etc) and setting in motion the project process through planning. This setting in its inherent collaborative nature calls for successful networking between the project stakeholders comprised of users, developers and decision makers in the organization. These stakeholders bring to the engagement not only their interests but also attitudes that should inform the ways to achieve a level playing field. Successful establishment is achieved in the background of a mutual understanding of the problem and of the process to the solution characterized by the stakeholders achieving consensus with respect to their represented interests and the inherent context characteristics they find themselves in.

Carrying out the project establishment as described above enabled the project stakeholders to buy into the project ideas and activities resulting in the formation of a project network. The network can be considered a social phenomenon that involves the stakeholders relating to one another in the context of a project in various ways. Moreover, the relations are further influenced by the contextual issues in which the network finds itself in. In this regard it is possible to identify this phenomenon as consisting of an interaction between the project establishment context issues (both from the stakeholders and from the situation in the organizations – e.g. processes, the structure and modes of working) and the engagement process that is adopted for the project establishment exercise. The context issues end up influencing the engagement approach adopted. This consequently means the approach ends up influencing the context issues **(Figure 29)** as the establishment exercise progresses.

Figure 29: Relation of the context issues and the engagement approach

My propositions can be considered as promoting such a cyclic interplay as the contextual realities reconcile with the process. The contextual realities are observed in the stakeholders' attitudes, perspectives, ways of working, etc.

6.5.2. Fit into a cyclic and iterative process

A project establishment exercise seeks to among other things identify relevant features and objects in the target organization. These are used to create a representation of the problem and the accompanying mapping of that to a technical solution. Given the presented cyclic nature of the relation between the context issues and the engagement approach, any artifact representation that is created has a dynamic characteristic as well **(Figure 30)**. From an iteration in which for example an approach has lead to changes in the context issues, a new representation of the problem and the solution is expected. Consider for example the case where through promotion of empowerment ideals, the stakeholders change their perspectives on the context and therefore the representation of the future work processes changes. This will result in changes to any earlier generated technical mapping of such a process in the form of a (requirements or design) document. This means that the described approach directly supports the iterative nature of design methodologies through which various versions are generated in the process.

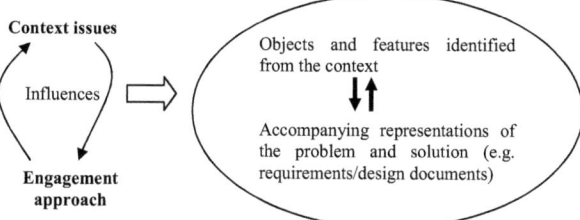

Figure 30: Cyclic production of establishment results

An example of objects, features and accompanying representations is a requirements document from the requirements analysis phase. From this discussion it follows that such a document will be iteratively generated. Further iterations are understood as manifestations of attempts at capturing the 'real world representations' from the evolving context. The document does not only represent observed realities but it has also the value of capturing and representing a "common referent" for the different conceptual spaces that the stakeholders bring to the process. It is a manifestation that the stakeholders are achieving a deep acquaintance with the project and pursuing a common goal. The results of the iterations also signify the level to which the project stakeholders are finding identity with each other and with the process. That is, assuming states of resonance with each other and the project establishment methods. Such a process in a developing country setting supports learning as proposed in Reflective Steps (Biru 2008). This leads to the argument that the resonance facilitators described here are only effective when embedded in a cyclic and iterative process such as proposed in STEPS.

6.5.3. Implication in contexts undergoing transformations

In the context of project establishment in a resonance seeking way, as described in this study, new levels of consciousness are created leading to new perspectives and new forms of knowledge. This is experienced in the emerging project process and, when integrated into the daily experiences of the individuals, they are likely to be reflected in activities beyond the project. This points to a state of transformation that is very much pronounced in developing countries' contexts where information system projects are embedded in broader change-oriented reform agendas.

6.6. Conclusion and further work

From a specific focus on power issues as defining unique characteristics of a context, this study has provided a contribution towards contextualized information systems development methodologies. The hypothesis confirmed is that when PD is applied in a developing country set up where the concepts of freedom (including freedom of expression), democratic principles at work places, forums for initiating dialogue and opportunities for learning are absent (or at least not as explicitly available as in the developed countries), then the focus of PD engagement approaches needs to change. The change is proposed in terms of pursuing the establishment of resonance amongst project stakeholders by way of enriching existing PD approaches to focus on addressing issues specific to an application context. Methods and techniques to facilitate bonding, coaching, achievement of learning and moderation have been presented based on empirical experiences in the Kenyan health sector during project establishment.

The general thrust of the proposed resonance facilitators lies in the recognition that a project team tasked to establish a project must develop a concerted effort to achieve mutual understanding and consensus on ideas to the extent that their interests are negotiated to reinforce the accomplishment of the other partners' interests. To achieve consensus on ideas, it is necessary to devise techniques that relate to the context's main issues especially that which support the narrowing of the gaps reflected in the participants' divergent power positions, interests and backgrounds. The propositions I have made are based on ideas from organizational structure and culture, political dimension of empowerment and workplace democracy. The overall essence of the enrichments is seen as promotion of empowerment and learning. Since these ideas are not limited to information systems development, the results reported here will find resonance with project initiation efforts beyond information technology. I see a direct applicability of the results in international development work.

Future work

Whereas reflections from empirical experiences in the Kenyan health sector has informed the reflections reported in this study, further study is required to explore from an even broader perspective the issues this research has identified. One approach to this is a comparative perspective across several sectors to identify any similarities or differences across sectors as well the applicability of the propositions in sectors other than health. Extension of this to the East African region is envisioned. I propose that such a broader perspective should seek to come up with a model that further abstracts the results of this study by merging the disjointed findings from similar studies in Africa. These include the Dialogical Systems Design method and the Reflective Steps based on Namibian and Ethiopian contexts respectively.

A multi-disciplinary research set-up based on this research would further validate the results reported here by seeking to merge the concepts of power, interests and attitudes to historical realities of developing countries, such as aspects inherited from colonization. This would extend the propositions to especially cater for change processes and the ever-present reality of seeking identity in developing countries.

In describing the analysis of the health sector, I have introduced the concept of *"Interaction-moments"*. Whereas I have not further explored the concept in this study, I propose future work based on this concept as a basis for a model to guide strategies for defusing power relations in projects.

7. References

Adler, N.J. (1986): *International Dimensions of Organizational Behavior*, Kent Publishing Co.: Boston, Mass

Agar, M. (1980): "The Professional Stranger, An Informal Introduction to Ethnography", Academic Press

Allwood, J., (1995): Language, Communication and Social Activity: Towards an analysis of the Linguistic Communicative Aspects of Social Activities. Junefelt, K. (ed.) *Proceedings of the 14th Scandinavian Conference of Linguistics and the 8th Conference of Nordic and General Linguistics*, Gothenburg papers in theoretical linguistics no. 73, Department of Linguistics, Goteborg University, Stockholm

Andersen, N.E., Kensing, F., Lundin, J., Mathiassen, L., Munk-Madsen, A., Rasbech, M., & Sorgaard, P. (1990): *Professional systems development: Experience, ideas and action*. Prentice Hall, London, 1990

Anderson, J. A., (1994): Experiences Integrating Object-Oriented Analysis with Joint Application Development (JAD). *Proceedings of the First International Eurospace- Ada-Europe Symposium*. Published in Lecture Notes in Computer Science vol 887 Springer-Verlag, London, UK p. 509-521

Argyris, C., Putnam, R., & McLain Smith, D. (1985): Action science: concepts, methods, and skills for research and intervention. San Francisco: Jossey-Bass

Asaro, P. M. (2000): "Transforming Society by Transforming Technology: The Science and Politics of Participatory Design." *Accounting, Management and Information Technologies*, Special Issue on Critical Studies of Information Practice, 10: 257-290

Ataöv, A. & Haider, J. (2006): "From Participation to Empowerment: Critical Reflections on a Participatory Action Research Project with Street Children in Turkey." *Children, Youth and Environments* 16(2): 127-152

Atkinson, P. (1990): *The Ethnographic Imagination: Textual Constructions of Reality*. London: Routledge

Avgerou C. (1996): Transferability of information technology and organizational practices. In: Odedra-Straub (Ed.) *Global information technology and socio-economic development*, Ivy League, New Hampshire: p. 106-115

Avgerou, C., Ciborra, C., Land, F. F., (eds) (2004): *The Social Study of Information and Communications Technology: Innovation, Actors and Context*, OUP Oxford

Avison D., Lau F., Myers M.. & Nielsen, P.A. (1999): Action Research, *Communications of the ACM*, 42 (1): p. 94- 97

Avison, D. & Pries-Heje, J. (2005): *Research in Information Systems: A Handbook for Research Students and Their Supervisors*. Elsevier Butterworth-Heinemann: Oxford (Great Britain)

Balka, E. (2003): Getting the big picture: The macro-politics of information system development in a Canadian hospital. *Methods of Information in Medicine*, 21(4): p. 324-330

Bardram, J., (2000): "Scenario-based design of cooperative systems redesigning a hospital information system in Denmark", *Group decision and negotiation*, vol. 9: p. 237-250

Beck, E. E. (2002): "P for Political - Participation is Not Enough", Scandinavian Journal of Information Systems (14): p. 77-92

Bellman, L., Bywood, C. & Dale, S. (2003). Advancing working and learning through critical action research: creativity and constraints, *Nurse Education in Practice* Volume 3 (4): p. 186-194

Beltrán, L. R., (1975): "Research Ideologies in Conflict". *Journal of Communication*. Vol 25: p. 187-193

Beltrán, L. R., (1980): "A Farewell to Aristotle: 'Horizontal' Communication". *Communication* Vol 5: p. 5-41

Biru, T. (2008): Reflective Steps. PhD Thesis at Department of Informatics, Hamburg University

Bjerknes, G. & T. Bratteteig (1995): User Participation and Democracy. A Discussion of Scandinavian Research on System Development, *Scandinavian Journal of Information Systems*, vol 7(1): p. 73-98

Bødker, S., (2000): Scenarios in user-centred design – Setting the stage for reflection and action. *Interacting with computers*, Vol 13(1): p. 61-75

Boudourides, M. A. (2001): The Politics of Technological Innovations: Network Approaches," paper presented at the *International Summer Academy on Technological Studies: User Involvement in Technological Innovation*, Deutschlandsberg, Austria

Braa, J., Hanseth, O., Mohammed, W., Heywood, A., & Shaw, V. (2007): Developing Health Information Systems in Developing Countries. The Flexible Standards Strategy. *MIS Quarterly* Vol 31(2): p. 381-402

Bratteteig, T. (2003): Making change: Dealing with relations between design and use. PhD. Thesis Department of Informatics, University of Oslo

Brooks, F.P. J. (1987): No Silver Bullet Essence and Accidents of Software Engineering. *Computer*, vol.20 (4): p.10-19

Cabrera, Á., Cabrera E. F., & Barajas, S. (2001): The key role of organizational culture in a multi-system view of technology-driven change International. *Journal of Information Management*, Volume 21(3): p. 245-261

Callon M. (1986a): Some elements of a sociology of translation: Domestication of the scallops and the fishermen of St Brieuc Bay. In: Law, J. (ed.) *Power, action and belief*, Routledge and Kegan Paul London: p. 196-233

Callon, M. (1986b): The sociology of an Actor Network: The case of the electric vehicle. In M. Callon, J. Law & A. Rip (eds.), *Mapping the Dynamics of Science and Technology: Sociology of Science in the Real World*. Macmillan London: p. 19-34

Carroll, J.M. & Rosson, M.B. (2007): Participatory design in community informatics Design Studies. Vol 28 (3): p. 243-261

Casalegno, F. & McWilliam, I. M., (2004): Communication Dynamics in Technological Mediated Learning Environments. *International Journal of Instructional Technology and Distance Learning* Vol 1(11): p. 15-33

Chambers, R. (1997): *Whose reality counts? Putting the first last* (2nd ed.). ITDG Publishing Colchester, UK

Cherns, A., (1976): The Principles of Sociotechnical Design, in *Human Relations,* Vol 2(9): p. 783-792

Christel, M. G. & Kang K. C. (1992): Issues in Requirements Elicitation, Technical Report: CMU/SEI-92-TR-012 ESC-TR-92-012

Chung, L., Hung, F., Hough, E., Ojoko-Adams, D., & Mead, N. R., (2006): Security Quality Requirements Engineering. Case Study Phase III. SPECIAL REPORT CMU/SEI-2006-SR-003

Clarkson, M.B.E. (1995): A stakeholder framework for analyzing and evaluating corporate social performance. *Academy of Management Review, Vol* 20(1): p. 92-117

Clegg, C.W. (2000): Sociotechnical Principles for Systems Design, in *Applied Ergonomics*, Vol. 31: p. 463-477

Clement, A. and P. Van den Besselar (1993): A Retrospective Look at PD Projects. In M. Muller and S. Kuhn (eds.): *Participatory Design: Special Issue of the Communications of the ACM*, vol. 36(4): p. 29-39

Cockburn A. (2003): People and Methodologies in Software Development. PhD Thesis at the Faculty of Mathematics and Natural Sciences, University of Oslo, Norway

Colucci, W. (2003): Structural factors in information system success: Limits and possibilities of 'project leadership', 'participation' 'commitment'" in *Proceedings of the annual meeting of the International Communication Association*, San Diego, CA

Cortes S. & Carlos E. (1997): Communication at the pace of the pendulum: a half-century in quest of development. In *Communication for Social Change Anthology: Historical and Contemporary Readings,* Gumucio A. D., Tufte, T., Published by CFSC Consortium, Inc: p. 578-585

Dahms, M., & Faust-Ramos, E. (2002): Development from within: Community Development, Gender and ICTs. In *Feminist Challenges in the Information Age*, C. Floyd, G. Kelkar, S. Klein-Franke, C. Kramarae, C. Limpangog, Eds. Leske+Budrich, Opladen: p. 203-222

Dewey, J. (1991): *Logic: The Theory of Inquiry*. Carbondale: Southern Illinois University.

Ehn, P., & Kyng, M. (1987): The collective resource approach to systems design. In Bjerknes, G., Ehn, P., & Kyng, M. (Eds.), Computers and democracy: A Scandinavian challenge, Aldershot, UK: p. 17-57.

Elfrey, P., (2000): Physics, communication theory and the interactive world of experience-based entertainment and simulation: The Importance of resonance. *Proceedings of Summer Computer Simulation Conference*, Vancouver, Canada

Ellen, R. F. (ed.) (1984): *Ethnographic Research: A Guide to General Conduct*, London: Academic Press

Ellingsen G, Monteiro E. (2003): Big is Beautiful: electronic patient records in large Norwegian hospitals 1980s-2001. *Methods of Information in Medicine*, vol 42: p. 366-70.

Fals-Borda, O. (2001): Participatory (action) research in social theory: Origins and challenges. In *Handbook of action research*, P. Reason & H. Bradbury, Eds. Sage, London: p. 27-37

Faust–Ramos, E. (1999): *Autonomy and emancipatory ways of learning and using information technologies*. Research report of Departmento de informatica e Estatistica, Universidade Federal de Santa Catalina. Florianopolis.

Fetterman, D. M. (1998): *Ethnography*, 2nd edition. Sage Publications, Thousand Oaks, CA.

Flicker,S., Savan, B., McGrath, M., Kolenda, B. & Matto M.. (2007): 'If you could change one thing. . .' What community based researchers wish they could have done differently. *Community Development Journal*, Oxford University Press. Vol 43: p. 239 – 253

Floyd C., Reisin, F., & Schmidt, G. (1989a): STEPS to Software Development with Users. *In Lecture Notes in Computer Science, ESEC'89 2nd European Software Engineering Conference*, C. Ghezzi, J. McDermid, Eds. University of Warwick, UK, 11-15

Floyd, C., Mehl, M., Reisin, F-M., Schmidt, G., & Wolf, G., (1989b): "Out of Scandinavia: Alternative Software Design and Development in Scandinavia." In: *Journal for Human-Computer-Interaction*. Lawrence Erlbaum Ass, Hillsdale, N.J.Vol.4: p. 253-380

Freire P. (1993): *Pedagogy of the oppressed*. Continuum Books, New York

Freire, P. (1970): *Pedagogy of the Oppressed*. Continuum Publishing ,New York

Freire, P. (1973): *Extension or Communication*. The Seabury Press, New York

Galliers, R. (1992): "Choosing Information System Research Approaches," in Galliers, R. (ed.), *Information System Research: Issues, Methods and Practical Guidelines*, Blackwell Scientific Publications, Oxford: p. 144-162

Gärdenfors P., (1996): "Human communication: what happens?" in Reichert, B. (eds) *The Contribution of Science and Technology to the Development of Human Society*, ECSC-EC-EAEC, Brussels. (The article is published on the accompanying CD-ROM as document C2-1A.pdf).

Gärdenfors, P. (2004): Cooperation and the evolution of symbolic communication. In Oller, K. and Griebel, U. (Eds.) *The Evolution of Communication Systems*, MIT Press, Cambridge, MA: p. 237-256

Gärtner, J. & Wagner I. (1996): Mapping Actors and Agendas: Political Frameworks of Systems Design and Participation. *Human-Computer Interaction*, vol. 11(3): p. 187–214

Giddens A. (1986): *The Constitution of Society: Outline of the Theory of Structuration*, University of California Press; Reprint edition ISBN 0-520-05728-7

Glaser, B, Strauss, A. (1967): The Discovery of Grounded Theory: Strategies for Qualitative Research, Aldine de Gruyter, NY

Greenbaum J. & Kyng M. (1996): *Design at work: cooperative design for computer systems*. Lawrence Erlbaum Associates, Hillsdale (NJ)

Greenwood, D. & Levin, M. (1998): Introduction to Action Research: Social Research for Social Change. Sage, California

Grills, S. (ed.) (1998): *Doing Ethnographic Research: Fieldwork Settings*, Sage Publications, Thousand Oaks, CA

Hall, H.H. (1987): *Organizations: Structure, processes, and outcomes*. (Fourth Ed.): Prentice-Hall, Englewood Cliffs, NJ

Hammersley, M. & Atkinson P. (1983): *Ethnography: Principles in Practice*. Routledge, London

Heeks, R. (2002): Information Systems and Developing Countries: Failure, Success, and Local Improvisations", *The Information Society* Vol. 18: p.101-112

Hofstede, G. (1991): *Cultures and organizations- Software of the mind*. McGraw Hill International

Huesca, R., (1995): A procedural view of participatory communication: Lessons from Bolivian tin miners' radio. *Media, Culture and Society,* Vol17 (1): p. 101-119

Huesca, R., (2003): From modernization to participation: The past and future of development communication in media studies. In A. N. Valdivia, (ed.), *A companion to media studies,* Blackwell Publishing: p. 50-71

Hult, M., & Lennung, S. (1980): "Towards a Definition of Action Research: A Note and Bibliography," *Journal of Management Studies* Vol 17(2): p. 242-250

Israel, B., Eng, B., Schulz, A., & Parker E. (Eds.) (2003): *Methods in community based participatory research methods,* Jossey-Bass San Francisco

Jones, P.H. (1997): *Handbook of team design: a practitioner's guide to team system development*. Mc Graw-Hill

Kanstrup, A. M. (2003): D for democracy: on political ideals in participatory design. *Scandinavian Journal of Information Systems* Vol 15 (1): p. 81-85

Kaplan B. (1997): Addressing organizational issues into the evaluation of medical systems. *Journal of the American Information Association* Vol 4: p. 94-101

Keen, P. G. (1981): Information systems and organizational change. *Communications of the ACM* Vol 24 (1): p. 24-33

Kensing, F., Simonsen, J., Bødker, K. (1996): MUST - A method for Participatory Design In *Proceedings of the Fourth Biennial Conference on Participatory Design*, CPSR

Kensing, F., & Blomberg, J. (1998): Participatory Design: Issues and Concerns. *Computer Supported*

Keyton, J., (2005): *Communication & Organizational Culture: A Key to Understanding Work Experiences*. Sage Publications, Thousand Oaks, CA

Khandwalla, P.N. (1977): "Some top management styles, their context and performance", *Organization and Administrative Sciences* Vol, 7 (4): p. 21-51.

Kilburg, R. R., (1996): Towards a conceptual understanding and definition of executive coaching, *Consulting Psychology Journal*, Vol 48 (2): p. 134-44

Kim D. (2000): Corporate Citizenship: A Stakeholder Approach for Defining Corporate Social Performance and Identifying Measures for Assessing It. *Business & Society*, Sage Publications, Inc. Vol. 39 (2): p. 210-219

Kiura, S. M. (2006): Project Establishment in the Context of Participatory Design: Experience from a Hospital Information System Development Project in a Developing Country. In *Proceedings of the 39th Annual Hawaii international Conference on System Sciences* (HICSS). IEEE Computer Society, Washington, DC, Vol 5

Kiura, S., Hornetz, K. J., (2007): ICT in the Kenya Health SWAp Process: A Development Partner's Experiences and Perspectives - *proceedings of the 8th Annual ICT Conference Strathmore University*, Nairobi, Kenya

Krabbel, A., Wetzel, I. (1997): "Vorgehensweise bei der Auswahl eines integrierten Krankenhausinformationssystems", In: Köhler, C.O., Ellsässer, K.-H. (Hrsg.) Medizinische Dokumentation und Information - Handbuch für Klinik und Praxis. Loseblattsammlung, ecomed, Landsberg: I-5

Krause, D., Rolf, A., Christ, M., and Simon, E. (2006): Wissen, wie alles zusammenhangt, *Informatik-Spektrum*, Vol29(4): p. 263–273

Latour, B. (1987): *Science in Action*. Harvard University Press, Cambridge, MA

Latour, B. (1988): The Prince for machines as well as for machinations. In B. Elliott (ed.), *Technology and Social Process*. Edinburgh University Press, Edinburgh: p. 20-43

Law, J. (1988): The anatomy of a socio-technical struggle: The design of the TSR2. In B. Elliott (ed.), *Technology and Social Process*. University Press, Edinburgh: p. 44-69

Law, J. (1991): Introduction. In J. Law (ed.), *A Sociology of Monsters: Essays on Power, Technology and Domination*. Routledge, London & New York: p. 1-23

Leavitt, H.J (1965): *Applying organizational change in industry: Structural, technological and humanistic approaches. Handbook of Organizations*, J.G. March, Ed. Rand McNaily, Chicago, IlL

Lee J. (2008): Determinants of government bureaucrats' new PMIS adoption: the role of organizational power, it capability, administrative role and attitude. *The American Review of Public Administration*, Vol. 38(2): p.180-202

Lorenzi N.M., Riley R.T., Blyth A.J.C., Southon G., & Dixon B.J. (1997): Antecedents of the people and organizational aspects of medical informatics, review of the literature. *JAM Med Inform Assoc* Vol 4: p. 79-93

Lyytinen, K. (1987): A taxonomic perspective of IS development: theoretical constructs and recommendations", in Boland, R.J., Hirschheim, R. (Eds),*Critical Issues in Information Systems Research*, Plenum, New York, NY.

Markus, M. L., & Robey, D. (1988): Information technology and organizational change: causal structure in theory and research, Management Science, Vol. 34(5): p. 583-598

Martin J., Siehl C. (1983): "Organizational Culture and Counterculture: An Uneasy Symbiosis," *Organizational Dynamics*, Vol 2: p. 52-64

Mathiassen L., (1997): Reflective Systems Development, Submitted as Dr. Tech. Thesis, Aalborg University

Mathiassen, L. (2000): Collaborative Practice Research. In: *Organizational and Social Perspectives on Information Technology*. R. Baskerville, J. Stage & J. I. DeGross (Eds.), Kluwer Academic Publishers

Matthiassen, L. (1998): "Reflective systems development". *Scandinavian Journal of Information Systems* Vol 10 (issue 1&2): p. 67-118

Maxwell, J. A., & Loomis D., (2002): Mixed methods design: An alternative approach. In *Handbook of mixed methods in social and behavioral research*, edited by Tashakkori A. & Teddlie C. Sage, Thousand Oaks, CA: p. 241–271

Middleton P. (1999): "Managing information system development in bureaucracies" *Information and Software Technology*, vol. 41: p. 473-482

Mikkelsen, B. (1995: *Methods for development Work and research. A guide for practitioners.* Sage publications, New Delhi

Mintzberg, H. (1978): Patterns in strategy formulation. *Management Science,* Vol 24(9): p. 934–948

MoH. (2007): A situational analysis study of the faith based health services vis-à-vis the government health services: A Report of the Ministry of Health and Faith Based Health Services Technical Working Group

Mosar, C. (1993): *Gender Planning and Development. Theory, Practice and Training.* Routledge, London

Mursu, A.; Soriyan, H.A.; Olufokunbi, K.; Korpela, M. (2000): "Information systems development in a developing country: theoretical analysis of special requirements in Nigeria and Africa,", *2000. Proceedings of the 33rd Annual Hawaii International Conference on System Sciences.* Vol. 7

Myers, M. D. (1997): "Qualitative Research in Information Systems," MIS Quarterly Vol 21(2): p. 241-242

Myers, M. D. (1999): "Investigating Information Systems with Ethnographic Research," *Communications of the Association for Information Systems*, Vol 2(23): p. 1-20

Nyce, J. M. & Bader, G. (2002): On foundational categories in software development. In *Social Thinking: Software Practice*, Y. Dittrich, C. Floyd, & R. Klischewski, Eds. MIT Press, Cambridge, MA: p. 29-4

Oliver, D. (2003): Technology, Language and Power in ERP adoption Central Queensland University. In *Proccedings of Critical management studies track*, L. Oliver, C. Romm, Eds. Lancaster University, England

Orlikowski W.J. (1993): CASE Tools as Organizational Change: Investigating Incremental and Radical Changes in Systems Development. MIS Quarterly, Vol 17 (3): p. 309-340

Orlikowski W.J., Walsham G, Jones M.R., DeGross J.I. eds. (1995): Information technology and changes in organizational work *proceedings of the IFIP WG8.2 working conference on information technology and changes in organizational work*. Chapman & Hall, London

Orlikowski, W. J. (2000): Using technology and constituting structures: a practice lens for studying technology in organizations. *Organization Science*. Vol 11(4): p. 404-428

Oyaya, C. O. & Rifkin, S. B. (2003): Health sector reforms in Kenya: an examination of district level planning. *Health Policy*, Elsevier, vol. 64(1): p. 113-127

Peel, V., (2005): The significance of behavioral learning theory to the development of effective coaching practice. *International Journal of Evidence Based Coaching and Mentoring* Vol. 3(1)

Porto de Albuquerque, J., Simon, E.J. (2007): Dealing with Socio-Technical Complexity: Towards a transdisciplinary approach to IS research. In: Hubert Österle, Joachim Schelp, Robert Winter (Eds.), Proceedings of the 15th European Conference on Information Systems (ECIS 2007): p. 1458-1468

Pouloudi, A. (1997): 'Stakeholder Analysis as a Front-End to Knowledge Elicitation', *AI & Society*, Vol 11: p. 122-137

Rapoport, R.N. (1970): "Three Dilemmas in Action Research," *Human Relations* Vol 23 (6): p. 499-513

Reddy, M., Pratt, W., Dourish, P., Shabat, M. (2003): "Socio-technical requirements analysis for clinical systems", *Methods of Information in Medicine* Vol. 42: p.437-44

Rolf, A. (2004): Von der Theoriearbeit zur Gestaltung. In Wissensgesellschaft. Neue Medien und ihre Konsequenzen. Bundeszentrale für politische Bildung, Bonn

Schein, E. H. (1996): Three cultures of management: The key to organizational learning. *Sloan Management Review*,. Vol 38(1): p. 9–20

Schön, D. A. (1983): The Reflective Practitioner: How Professionals Think in Action. Basic Books, New York

Schön, D. A. (1987): Educating the Reflective Practitioner, Toward a New Design for Teaching and Learning in the Professions. Jossey-Bass,San Francisco

Schreyögg, G., Sydow, J., and Koch, J. (2003): Organisatorische Pfade — von der Pfadabhängigkeit zur Pfadreaktion. Managementforschung, Wiesbaden Vol. 13

Sen, A.K. (2000): Development as freedom. Anchor Books, New York

Shipman, M. (1998): *The limitations of social research*, 3rd ed. Longman, London

Simon, E., Janneck, M., and Gumm, D. (2006): Understanding socio-technical change: Towards a multidisciplinary approach, In Social Informatics: An Information Society for all? In remembrance of Rob Kling, *Proceedings of the 7th International Conference Human Choice and Computers*. Springer: p. 469– 479

Smith, B. C. (1997): The decentralization of health care in developing countries: organizational options. *Public Administration and Development. Vol* 17: p. 399–412

Sommerville I. (2001): *Software engineering*. Addison-Wesley, San Francisco

St. Clair, R. N., (1999): Cultural Wisdom, Communication Theory, and the Metaphor of Resonance. In Davey W.G. (ed.), *Intercultural Communication Studies, Special Issue on Language and Interculturalism*. Institute for Cross-Cultural Research, USA Vol. 8 (1): p. 79-102

St. Clair, R.N., (2007): The Framework of Cultural Space. In *Proceedings of International Conference on Intercultural Communication. Harmony, Diversity and Intercultural Communication*, Harbin China

Suchman, L. (1993): Forward. In D. Schuler and A. Namioka (Eds.) *Participatory Design: Principles and Practices*. Lawrence Erlbaum, N.J. : p. vii–ix

Suomi, R (2000): Leapfrogging for modern ICT usage in the health care sector. In Hansen, Hans-Robert - Bichler, Martin - Mahrer, Harald (editors) *A Cyberspace Odyssey. Proceedings of the 8th ECIS conference*, Wien: p. 1269-1275

Thoresen, K.(1999): Computer Use, PhD thesis, University of Oslo

Timmons S. (2003): Resistance to computerized care planning systems by qualified nurses working in the UK NHS. *Meth Inf Med* Vol 42: p. 471-6

Tonnessen, T. (2005): Continuous innovation through company wide employee participation. The TQM Magazine. Emerald Group Publishing, Vol 17(2): p.195-207

Trice, H. M., & Beyer, J. M. (1993): The cultures of work organizations. Prentice Hall, Englewood Cliffs, NJ

UN Website. Millennium Development Goals. Available at: http://www.un.org/millenniumgoals Accessed December 2008

Waema T. M. (1996): Implementation of information technology projects and economic development: Issues, problems and strategies. In: Odedra-Straub (ed.) *Global information technology and socio-economic development,* Ivy League, New Hampshire: p. 106-115

Wallerstein, N. B. and Duran, B. (2006): Using Community-Based Participatory Research to Address Health Disparities. *Health Promotion Practice*, Vol. 7(3): p. 312-323

Walt, G., Pavignani, E., Gilson, L., Buse, K. (1998): Managing external resources in the health sector:

are there lessons for swaps? *Health Policy and Planning Vol* 14 (3): p. 273–284.

Wamai, R. G. (2000): NGO and Public Health Systems: Comparative Trends in Transforming Health Care Systems in Kenya and Finland. *International Society for Third Sector Research (ISTR) Sixth International Conference on "Contesting Citizenship and Civil Society in a Divided World* Ryerson University and York University Toronto, Canada

WHO. (2000): The world health report 2000: Health systems: Improving performance. Geneva: Author; distributed by the WHO Publications Center USA, Albany, N.Y

Winschiers, H. (2001): Dialogical systems design across cultural boundaries: system design out of Africa. PhD Thesis at Department of Informatics, Hamburg University

Wood, J. and Silver, D. (1995): *Joint Application Development* 2nd Edition. John Wiley & Sons, New York, 1995

World Bank. (2005): Paris declaration on aid effectiveness, Paris. Available from www1.worldbank.org/harmonization/paris/finalparisdeclaration.pdf

Yin, R. (1994): *Case study research: Design and methods* (2nd ed.). Sage Publishing, Thousand Oaks, CA

Zhang, M., J. McCullough & Y. W. Ren (2004): Effects of organizational Structure and Information Technology Capability in Emerging Market. *Journal of Academy of Business and Economics Vol. 3*

8. Appendix I: Project 1

The description of this project has the following structure:

- Origin of ideas and preparation before proceeding to the hospital
- Detours that I encountered until I 'settled' in the hospital
- Information about the hospital, including arguments why the hospital was suited for the research
- Interactions guide questions
- Highlights from the interactions in the sector
- Summary of the aims, associated problems and issues identified from the interactions

Preamble: Genesis of the project ideas

The idea to develop an integrated health information system for "Hillside" district in Kenya was coined in early 2003 while in Hamburg, Germany. Based on my experiences with the health system in Hamburg, the development of the health information system was to be part of my contribution to the development of the district by empowering the locals in the district to easily access health related information. I envisioned following the model of "information kiosks" strategically placed in various locations in the district from where the district citizens would have access to all-round health information. A component of the system was to have modules where the medical practitioners – doctors and nurses in the health centers and dispensaries in the district – would have possibilities to download to their own data carriers latest information about their profession as a means of keeping them abreast with advancements in health related information. The goal of the exercise was extended to include seeking achievement of empowerment of the locals, socio-justification of project, acceptance of the project and its sustainability by the users of the system in the long run. This lead to adoption of participatory methods as the most suited methodologies for carrying out the project. I joined the research group of software engineering at the University of Hamburg and registered my candidacy for a PhD Programme at the university based on these project ideas. As a concrete participatory design methodological approach, I selected a framework for evolutionary participatory software development. Expertise on the framework was readily available at the group, the framework having been developed by the chair of the software engineering group and colleagues (Floyd et. al 1989a).

Detours to "Hillside" Provincial General Hospital

Armed with knowledge of participatory design methods practice and having read about other experiences from other parts of the world as documented especially by Dahms and Faust-Ramos (2002), Faust–Ramos (1999), Mikkelsen (1995), Mosar, (1993), Mursu et al. (2000), I established contacts in the district. I left Hamburg for Kenya and headed to the district where he met the earlier established contacts and discussed the ideas of the system. From the discussions, it became clear that the administrative framework that was concerned with health information provision and implementation of health interventions in the district was understood as 'the hospital'. When it came to health related matters, the locals had no relation to the administrative offices at the county, municipal or even provincial administration structures. This was despite the fact that these administrative structures had health administrative offices. Nobody expected the government administrative structures to provide health related information. This scenario presented the first call to change the ideas. It meant the ideas of the project had to be aligned to the structures of the ministry of health as represented by the hospital in the district and not the administrative structures of the district as earlier envisioned. The hospital that forms the backbone and the central point of access and provision of health services in the district is the "Hillside" Provincial General Hospital (HPGH) that acts as the referral hospital for the district and surrounding regions. Other than referral services, locals also have access to the casualty department of the hospital for outpatient services.

Once at the hospital I was advised to get a research permit before the hospital administration could officially deal with me. This was only possible from the ministry headquarters in Nairobi. The health administrative offices at the district and the provincial administrative offices were not in a position to provide such a permit and both offices referred me to the ministerial headquarters. I was not receiving any cooperation without the permit and I had to travel to the ministry headquarters and seek for a research permit "... *or at least an introduction from our bosses ...*" as my partners at the hospital had put it. With this turn of events, I realized that the research and accompanying project ideas had to be embedded to a given department in the ministry headquarters. From studying the structure of the ministry, possible linkage department was found out to be the Health Management Information System (HMIS) department. I established contacts with this department at headquarters. It however emerged that this department existed neither at the district health administrative offices nor at the hospital. To maintain focus of the project intervention to the district, contacts to a department that had representation at the hospital and other health structures at the district was sought. The nearest shot was the department of health records and information that incidentally worked very closely with the HMIS department. This was represented as a department at the hospital and existed in the district and provincial health administrative and management offices. I presented my ideas to the department's senior staff who found them relevant and asked for my research proposal (the one presented for registration at the university in Hamburg). After a few days I got the research permit to present to relevant departments in "Hillside". Although the research permit was secured via the health records and information department, I maintained close contacts with the HMIS department as well, and consulted them as resource persons in the workshops and discussions at the district.

With this permit, I was back at the hospital and received excellent cooperation from the hospital management and other departments (not just the health records and information department). The project idea was extensively discussed with the hospital departments and reached a decision to limit the initial achievable aspects of the project to be directly related to the hospital operations. The hospital did not have ICT systems in place, meaning it was far fetched to plan for district level ICT systems when the nerve center of the district health operations did not have such systems in place. The capacity for running and using the initially conceived system was not available at the district. The hospital's department of health records and information became the direct counterpart of the research. I did an analysis of the needs at the hospital. The findings revealed that the practical first steps for a hospital information system was to involve reporting processes in the department whereby a system was needed to support the department's reporting obligations. These obligations turned out to be submission of reports to the departments of HMIS and health records and information at the headquarters. The initial system module was agreed to be a system to report on the morbidity and mortality information for the inpatient department; the electronic process beginning after manual indexing and coding of the discharge summaries from the wards.

About the hospital

The "Hillside" Provincial General Hospital (HPGH) is located in "Hillside" town, approximately 120 kilometers (75 miles) northeast of Nairobi towards Mount Kenya. "Hillside" town serves as the provincial headquarters of Eastern Province in Kenya and is also the district headquarters of "Hillside" District. Located on the southeastern slopes of Mount Kenya, the town of "Hillside" has a population of 41,092 (as of the latest official census of 1999) compared to the district's total population of about 300,000. The hospital is situated about 1 km from the town centre. It serves as a referral Hospital for Eastern Province as well as adjacent parts of Central Province. It is also a teaching and internship centre for medical universities and colleges in Kenya.

Size

The hospital has a bed capacity of 618 (444 beds and 174 cots). There are 17 admitting wards out of which two are amenity wards. Amenity wards provide single rooms in which patients enjoy privacy with self-contained rooms as opposed to the "standard" wards that are a dormitory style accommodating several patients in a large open room. The male amenity ward has a bed capacity of 16 beds while the female amenity ward has a bed capacity of 12 beds. The outpatient department is the biggest of the departments (serving as the casualty) housed in two blocks that nevertheless are normally heavily congested.

Whereas the hospital can be said to be a medium sized hospital, it has over 500 staff members. **Table 2** shows the staff establishment as reported in the hospital's annual report prepared in December 2007. Moreover, the hospital on average reports over 10,000 cases in a month.

Job titles	Staff establishment
Consultants	11
Medial Officers	11
Medical Officers intern	26
Dentists	1
Dentists technologists	3
Clinical Officers	24
Community oral health officers	1
Enrolled community nurses	222
Kenya Registered Community Health Nurses	73
Lab Technologists	12
Lab Technicians	16
Medical Engineering technologists	2
Medical Engineering Technicians	6
Artisans	5
Occupational therapists	9
Orthopedic technologists	3
Health records and information officers	1
Health records and information technicians	4
Pharmacists	3

Job titles	Staff establishment
Physiotherapists	10
Public Health technicians	2
Plaster technicians	8
Pharmacy Technologist	4
Radiographers	8
Nutritionists	5
Health Administrative Officers	3
Executive Officers	1
Drivers	5
Cooks	1
Supportive staff (ss)	41
Clerks	12
Mortuary attendants	0
Patient attendants	0
Security Officers	0
Copy Typist	1
Store Men	3
Personal secretary	1
Telephone Operators	3
Auxiliary Boiler Technician	1
Total personnel	**542**

Table 2: Staff establishment in the hospital

Organization and management of the hospital

The Hospital Management Team (HMT) is concerned with the day-to-day running of the hospital with the medical superintendent as the chairman. This team meets regularly for updates on routine activities and for planning. The team membership is drawn from each hospital department as shown in **Table 3**. Other than the management team there is also the Provincial Hospital Management Board (PHMB) that works in conjunction with the HMT, representing the health services consumers (and other sectors) as a means to oversee the general provision of health care in the district and the larger Eastern province. The PHMB members are appointed by the Minister for health and published in the official government gazette.

Representative	Position in the team
Medical Superintendent	Chairman
Hospital Administrative Officer	Secretary
Hospital Matron	Member
X-Ray in-charge	Member
Physiotherapist in-charge	Member
Occupational therapist in-charge	Member
Health Records Information Officer In-charge	Member
Medical Officers of various departments	Member
SOPC, MOPC, GOPC, POPC	Member
Officer in charge ENT	Member
Clinical Officer in charge	Member
Nutritionist in charge	Member

Representative	Position in the team
Dentist	Member
Pharmacist in charge	Member
Lab technologist in charge	Member
Various ward in charges	Member
Hospital maintenance in charge	Member

Table 3: Hospital Management Team (HMT) composition

Suitability of the hospital for the study

With the objective of the research being to study the application of a software development methodology in a specific context and make propositions for a contextualized methodological approach, the hospital is considered suited for the study for various reasons that include:

- The prevailing social dynamics under which this hospital operates are not foreign to the principal researcher. This is from previous interactions with the institution and being a member of the community under which the hospital's geographical area of jurisdiction falls.
- The study from the beginning was aware of cultural influences in the practice of participatory design. In this regard, the study sought to avoid inter-cultural issues and concentrated on close assessment of intra-cultural social issues as opposed to cross-cultural issues in contexts. The setting of this institution within a 'single culture' means the conflicts of imposing outside cultures are minimal. A core value of the presupposed intra-cultural setting was expected from the onset to be a major strength in analyzing the engagement with the participants and coming up with propositions that represented typical nature of work in the health sector.
- The interplay and interdependence of various health practitioners is well represented in this hospital. With its unique nature of serving as both a district as well as a provincial hospital, the diversity of involved practitioners, covered spectrum of health issues and the wide range of services offered it is a representative sample of the health provision activities in the country's public sector, featuring a direct link to the lower levels of the services provision (public facilities) and the national policy setting structures of the sector.
- The close ties it has to the Health ministry headquarters, especially the Health records and management information systems departments and the close co-operation with the ministry in information capture and reporting provides a fertile ground for studying common sector features vis-à-vis adoption of participative approaches.
- The hospital presents opportunities for the diffusion of the results to the sector (especially in the district) through the influence of its position in the health sector hierarchy and the positions of the represented staff cadres in the ministry of health. Moreover, the health centers and dispensaries, district and sub-district hospitals, private and NGO health canters, medical training schools, nursing and maternity homes in the district have reporting obligations via the hospital and get supplies from (or through) the hospital. This further makes the case that experience at the hospital's area of jurisdiction serves as a representative sample of the sector.

Overview of the project timeline

I was at the hospital for the purposes of this study at three different times shown in **Figure 31**. One month in September 2003, for four months from mid May 2004 to September 2004 and for one month from mid March 2005. During this time I did interviews and workshops at the hospital, at the district, provincial and national levels of the sector. See **Table 4** for a breakdown listing of these interactions. The workshops brought together the hospital representatives in a single forum, another brought together hospital administration and representatives from the district and provincial administration offices. In collaboration with the district medical officer of health I held a climax workshop for the entire district with representatives from the District Health Management Team (DHMT) and the hospital staff including administrative staff.

September 2003		May 2004 to September 2004		March 2005
Familiarization and to get the go ahead		Full time stay at the hospital acquiring the documented and reported experiences in this study		Review of the developed and deployed prototype and attempt to expand the scope of the project
	Arrangements for study funding and further preparations		Reflections and publication	

Figure 31: Overview of project time line

Introductory meeting with the hospital management
Introductory session with the health records and information department head
Informal interviews with health records and information staff + working at the department
Formal interview with head of health records and information department
Half day workshop with the whole health records and information department +HMIS tasks
Formal Interview – district physiotherapy department staff
Formal Interview – provincial orthopedic head and community quality service representative
Informal interview – physiotherapy, APDK, orthopedic and executive office staff
Informal interviews – Administration, Pharmacy, MCH, inpatient, outpatient, clinical officers
Workshop – "Data collection and analysis" with the all hospital departments represented
formal interview District medical officer of health
formal interview – head provincial health records and information
Informal interview – deputy provincial health records and information
Design workshop – health records and information staff +Administration
Formal interview Deputy chief health records and information officer
Formal interview – HMIS information design officer
Workshop, hospital, district and provincial teams with facilitation from headquarters (HMIS and health records departments)
Workshop – with the district health management team (DHMT)

Table 4: Breakdown of major interaction in the project

Interactions guideline

I can summarize my tasks during this time in as far as they relate to project establishment phase as having been about: Introductions to the health sector (preceded by a research design), getting a research permit, appraising the project context ('inventory' of people, projects and previous relevant projects), continuous communication of the project ideas, setting the scope, composing the project team, continuous design and prototype development work, carrying out duties (participation) at the health records and information department, maintaining a wide representation of the hospital departments and administrative offices – district and provincial levels.

These are tasks geared towards achieving my understanding of projects establishment that I present in this study. In my interactions (both the interviews and workshops) I had an outline that guided the proceedings. Here I summarize the main points of the guideline from which I adapted specific agenda items as necessary, both with individuals and groups.

- Self introductions: covering: where from, professional background, why him/her or the department/group, etc
- Introduction of the underlying ideals informing the research: Participatory design, computer supported collaborative work, knowledge management, promotion of using information resources in the sector, potential of ICTs in enhancing service delivery, self motivation to contribute to development with a focus on improving health indicators, search for solutions founded on sustainability, affordability, socio-economic justification and community participation, etc
- Statement of my expectations in the meeting and from the collaboration with the person/group which always included "to know you, what you do, where and how"
- Questions on the general state of affairs as the point of departure from actual work situations (to bring out specific features of their work such as continuity, iteration, cooperation, collaboration, etc)
- Questions on organizational structure (including departments, interactions, communication paths and reporting chains), ICT landscape (inventory of existing uses of technologies, support to immediate responsibilities, relevance/recognition of information value) and own evaluation of their state of data and collected information (dissemination experiences, formalization efforts, knowledge management and any positive experiences from such efforts)
- Views and perspectives on ICT driven services provision in their area of jurisdiction. Bringing out the vision of the way forward as indications of efforts for an integrated ICT supported services provision
- Views on sustainability and acceptance of projects oriented towards ICT use and what learning has been captured from past endeavors, proposed views on how to incorporate/achieve and maximize the likelihood for achieving long-term solutions in the sector
- Reasons for any negative experiences and the final status of what happened to the experiences (success, failure, changed focus/scope, etc)
- Invitation to evaluate and critique my ideas and more importantly how we can work together (given synergies not obvious in my ideas) on the way forward

In the interactions I was in search of specific answers in addition to setting the stage for collaboratively developing the system. My engagements in the project were informed by my understanding of project establishment as involving (in an iterative way) the processes of need identification, need analysis, communication of idea/s to address the need, gaining a commitment through resources provisions and setting in motion the process to address the need through planning.

Case story

At the hospital

I started with an introductory meeting with the hospital management where I was introduced in a meeting of heads of departments. I was received well and all were in agreement that the best department to be embedded in was the health records and information department that they described as the information hub of the hospital. It emerged that this department was also considered the 'IT department' of the hospital. The department staffs were perceived to be well versed with computers, preparing reports with a computer and assisting the administration/management when faced with computer related problems. Having explained the project ideas and the envisioned participative nature of the research, the message from the management was that all should take part. Everybody was motivated to enhance service delivery at the hospital and believed ICT had a part to play. Further clarifications came along in repeated meetings with the heads of departments and by my becoming 'a member of staff' at the records department. At the time of the study, the department had 5 staff members. The head and four others whose responsibilities were as follows: one was assigned to the inpatient department (including maternity), one was handling outpatient and the other two alternatively serving the front desk and "back office" work of indexing, archiving and retrieving patients' folders plus other daily clerical duties. I worked with all the sections and accompanied the head in various meetings.

Telecommunication infrastructure

The department collects, aggregates and reports data from all the hospital activities and therefore has direct working relations with all the departments and sections of the hospital. The department however primarily reports to the headquarters, specifically to the departments of health records and information and the health management information systems. It also keeps the district and provincial health administrative offices informed by way of copies of all reports sent to headquarters. These offices also make reporting requests to the department. The department had a single computer running windows 2000 professional and MS office 2000 professional with no health data reporting application. The department did not have a computer operator. This computer was used for preparing and compiling reports using Microsoft office applications (mainly excel and word). Other than the ad hoc requested reports, there are regular reports expected from the department on monthly, quarterly and annul basis. The department offices had no telephone connection – the whole hospital had a single functional direct telephone line connection. Someone wishing to make a telephone call required to get an authorization from the executive office and make the call from the hospital head's office. Internet and email connections were also unavailable at the department. Only the hospital head's office had a dial up connection (via the only functional telephone line).

Reporting processes
Having been embedded in the health records and information department one of my first endeavors was to get to know the activities of the department. From meetings with the department staff, including the head of the department, I was informed of the processes that form the department's work. This included a detailed description of how data collection starts from the patient consultation rooms. The clinical officers tally the cases diagnosed during patient consultations in provided tally sheets. These sheets are then forwarded to the health records department. Other than from the hospital, dispensaries and health centers in the district must submit to the department their duly filled tally sheets for each month by the 5th of the following month. A compiled report for the district is then prepared and must reach the headquarters by 21st of the month. The district and provincial administrative heads are sent copies and their mandate includes raising questions (to coordinate reporting – e.g. follow up in the event that reports are not submitted in time).

Another set of data processed at the department is from the inpatient department of the hospital. Each patient in the wards has a folder where all relevant entries are made. These folders remain at the wards with the patient until discharge or death. A discharge summary is made and the folder is sent to the health records department. At the records department, these folders are reorganized, coded, indexed and a summary is prepared. This involves making entries in separate 'cards' (MoH 268 form) for each disease. Reports are prepared from these cards on a quarterly basis (every 3 months). These folders are then filed (archived) and are retrieved in re-visit cases where the patient is re-admitted and/or presents a copy of the discharge summary sheet in a follow up visit to the hospital. A similar process is used for the maternity ward and birth notification records are forwarded to the district registrar of persons. The department also aggregates immunization data from the district (the hospital and all other dispensaries and health centers in the district) for the Kenya Expanded Programme on Immunization (KEPI).

Another major responsibility of the department is to coordinate the so-called 'special clinics'. These are cases where certain patients are under recurrent attention and are asked to visit the hospital repeatedly at intervals determined by the doctors. There are specific days of the week when the clinics are held at the hospital. The department is responsible for issuing registration forms and making bookings for the patients informing them of the days and times they should report to the consultants. The consultants are medical officers (doctors and clinical officers) working at the hospital. The dispensaries and health centers are also able to refer patients to the hospital for ailments diagnosed at those facilities. Special clinics are a part of the hospital's referral services.

The department reports on the workload of the health services in the district. This means the monthly number of outpatients visiting the health facilities as well as the district inpatient statistics such as number of occupied beds. These reports are forwarded to the headquarters – specifically to the heath records and information department, eventually ending up with the health management information system department for preparing a country-wide report. This report is published every three years. With the shortage of personnel and overwhelming increase in the number of patients visiting the hospital, the dispensaries and health centers, there was a huge backlog in reports and the department staffs were on average working 10 hours a day. The department head once said: *"Staffing, including hiring of casuals that would help in clerical tasks in the department is done from the chief executive office. Otherwise it is upon the headquarters to post more staff here. This department has no control or influence in securing such extra staff. Somebody who is aware of the problems we have in preparing the reports and the workload figures we report should be able to post more staff here"*. Other than the above reporting obligations, there are also ad hoc reporting requests that come from the headquarters or district and provincial health offices. The contents and depth necessary for such reports are included in the requests. The department has no influence on these demands and must comply necessitating working more hours in such situations. In some cases, someone is sent to the department from headquarters to 'supervise' preparation of such reports – this means long hours poring through huge amounts of paper work. Changes to reporting procedures and format, reporting timeframes, etc are devised at headquarters and communicated to the department as need arises.

The staffs at the hospital were aware of ICT's potential to improve on their work but from previous experiences, it was for them not clear how. A previous project had been conceived to interconnect all hospital departments to allow fast exchange of data between the various hospital departments. This failed upon realization that only 4 departments had computers (records, hospital head's office, accounts and the pharmacy departments). Such a project was a demonstration of top-down planning for the hospital by external management that missed the point of actual hospital needs. In informal discussions, an expressed fear for the project was that it was about young computer experts from headquarters sent to expose the operations at the hospital with the aim to victimize staff for failures and introduce new working and reporting responsibilities. Such fears became clearer in later design meetings. For example we had a departmental meeting with an officer from the HMIS (whom I had invited for insights to explain the reporting procedures). The meeting was tense and became more of supervisor issuing instructions on how things ought to be done. Other staffs who I expected to be the most resourceful (since they are the ones who actually do the work) were silent. Later when I questioned a colleague why he hadn't been of input in a design meeting where we had discussed a process which he happened to master it so well, he explained that *"in this ministry, you open up at your own risk. We deliver reports from the inpatients and maternity as required, but we don't necessary follow the process of recording to the letter. People at headquarters don't understand the community here. In the* (design) *meeting, you asked what is supposed to be done, not what we do!"*

For me to come up with a system that supported their actual work processes, I needed to get an understanding of the processes. At this time, it was not clear to me the difference between what was being done and what was supposed to be done. As it turned out, the supervisors and even heads of departments when asked to describe the reporting processes, they had a different view from the actual officers who did the work. In my follow up meeting I asked them to sketch the process. On a flip chart, we had several 'versions' of the same process as the different staff contributed to the descriptions (thanks to my relatively neutral moderation). Eventually after a prolonged and very argumentative session, we agreed on a general process as the anticipated and generic process encompassing what the staffs were doing and what their supervisors believed was "what was supposed to be done".

After a departmental meeting in which it had been decided that I was to handle the preparation of over due morbidity and mortality report, I was caught unawares when the following day, all folders from the wards landed on my desk before indexing and coding of the discharge summary sheets had been done. It emerged that the understanding was that my handling of the report preparation meant I was supposed to do all what was related to getting the report done. The computer system I was describing and coming up with was to their understanding supposed to replace their experiences in indexing, coding and making entries in the official forms that report the returns from the wards. This institutionalization of what they knew had not been taken kindly. We had a discussion with the colleague handling inpatient folders where we detailed the process of reporting these returns. Form this I was able to explain that my prototype was only coming in after they have indexed and coded the discharge summary sheets; the reaction was a sign of relief with the comment *"so we also have a place in the computer world"*. I was at pains to exalt the invaluable knowledge they brought in the process from hands-on experiences gathered over the years. I enquired about the opportunities the staff have for continued professional development, which would include topics about the use of computers as tools and understand that just as for other tools a computer is only useful when backed by the skills of an expert. I was informed that "upgrade courses" are for the staff in the dispensaries and health centers, and this is organized by the district clinical officers (in the DHMT). They include sensitization lectures and other community events meant to address common health issues and promoting good health practices. This explained the gap I was experiencing between my assumptions based on experiences elsewhere and what I was actually finding out.

In another meeting that brought the records department and the hospital administration we sought to plan a workshop with wider representation and institute a forum for exchange in reviewing the existing operations. The key to participation was given as financial support to the participants in the form of "out of pocket" allowances that include reimbursement of incurred transport costs. The forums from which staffs would have the opportunity to gather experiences get dominated by heads and superiors irrespective of their lines of duty. The main motivation is the extra financial gain from such events and it doesn't matter someone repeatedly attends a course that only another staff member would have benefited from (given direct relevance to work duties).

Motivated to see the hospital fraternity takes part in the project with wide representation, I had formal interviews with representatives from the departments of physiotherapy, orthopedic, pharmacy, maternal child health (MCH), inpatient, outpatient, representatives of clinical officers, a representative of the hospital head and the head of a unit that handles patients' complains at the hospital. I was introduced by the head of the records department as "coming from the headquarters". It was only later that I was informed the introduction as coming from the ministry headquarters means a lot to the meeting. *"Those are the people who convene meetings to review how we work here."* Networks based on personal rapport were evident in the discussions that ensued. The representations from departments increased through mere personal telephone calls to colleagues whose presence (for inputs) was felt necessary as discussions progressed. It was clear to me that as far as the staffs were dealing with each other in the same hierarchy (and I had she my "from the headquarters title") they collaborated with one another very well. As discussions and questions about the actual activities of the departments were degenerating to describing problems, complexity and lack of technological support, I raised the question of whether there existed a blue print documenting the need for systems in the hospital. The response was categorical that as someone from the headquarters, I should have it in my bag. *"... otherwise probably there is one in the heads of the provincial offices and at headquarters..."* The participants were asked to understand themselves as contributors to a working reporting system and therefore to give their views about their responsibilities to do regular reporting. The response was indifference and a failure to conceptualize the collaborative nature of the hospital work that is to be supported by the system. *"... Our problems and nature of work is different, the records people don't understand, we are not enough to do our work, yet they want us to report. But anyway, that we do".* A clinical officer went on *"... I don't think we can do much here, for example we are supposed to tally diagnosed cases in the MOH 701[2] form and we do that. We don't have a problem with that only that some times it's hard to correctly generalize sicknesses like in the MOH 701 list. The ministry should really think of how specific the information they want should be."* I was invited to "the field" to see for myself. *"... don't just stay at the hospital or the district and provincial offices, come and see what workloads we are talking about."* It emerged that the tools and reporting formats from the headquarters were not to be questioned or adapted to the actual local situation of the served community. This caused disincentive in the reporting exercise and the submission of huge reports that included irrelevant sections because the headquarters was not willing to have them left out.

Departments explained why earlier projects had failed with the arguments that the hospital needs medicines, not computers and efficiency is secondly to effectiveness. "Investments in technology are not a priority when we don't have a good delivery bed in the maternity". After lobbying to view ICT adoption as an enabler that would promote effectiveness and lessen their burden in carrying out the processes manually, the meeting identified other reasons for poor ICT diffusion in the hospital. These included lack of preference and understanding of the importance of data collection by their heads and not being clear about what exactly was expected in an IS for the health sector in the district. Absolving the heads of departments as the cause of these problems, I was advised to have a workshop with "bosses" from the district and provincial offices from which they are to view data and accompanying reporting differently. That was said to be the only way to get a useful system since the demands for follow-ups at the hospital arise from those "bosses". Further explanations for bad previous experiences were attributed to: *"our experiences don't count, headquarters are not ready to involve us, and our reports are up there, we have never heard of the reports follow-ups after we have sent them. On the other hand, once we have toiled so hard to provide information and report, we never get a response or see its contents reflected in the plans we get from above."* In this meeting I revisited the question I had struggled with long before I had a research permit as to why there is no IT department in the sector. One department head argued that *"...there is no IT department here not just because headquarters has not said we need one but also because there is no plan to make use of the information and content from such a department."*

Feedback from current information resources that would help in planning and monitoring of the activities was lacking. With this state of affairs, work was a routine and people wrote the reports because they were supposed to write without reflecting on the importance of their work. People didn't notice the relations of their work with their colleagues', including contributions in setting the agenda for the long term policy planning for delivery of health services in the district. For a situation in which work duties had become a routine (for example reporting exercise being oblivious to the value it has in informing and adding value to other colleagues' work), reflection that would enrich the duties got negatively affected. A collaborative and participative environment that fosters team work based on awareness of interfaces between one's tasks and the overall organizational goals and objectives was hindered. This only fostered misconception of

---

[2] MOH 701 form refers to a form that has a list of diseases on it. The list is supposed to feature all possible diseases and diagnosis that a clinical officer or any other health official making a diagnosis is likely to encounter

what ICT would do to help the situation and uninformed expectation that embracing an information system would be a panacea of all the problems hitherto experienced.

The meeting concluded that this would be appropriately addressed by having a feedback cycle that makes it clear how what is reported affects planning and consequently the reporter's future work. Systems should support people to see and feel the results of their work. It is not just about feedback from the top that is the problem but also the reporting officers do not follow up on their earlier reports. A case was narrated of how a former medical officer of health in Moyale district was transferred to Nairobi. Moyale is a district in the Northern Kenya region – a semi-arid area that is not only remote and poor, but also has very poor health indicators. Seven years later, he was the first one to open a report he had written while in Moyale. This was meant to be the 'most recent' information about the district. For him it was the same as if the report was arriving at the headquarters seven years later. Health indicators in the district had changed and continued use of such data as the current representation of the situation in the district was unfortunate. Health related data is within a month or two obsolete, irrespective of the source location. It seemed the people responsible for reporting had endorsed a situation in which their reports were heading to a bottomless inaccessible pit.

With respect to previous projects in the sector, several examples were given. One of these was the Kenya Quality Model (KQM) project that had been a national project targeted for all districts in Kenya and had included the delivery of computers to each district in the country. However, there was no reported use or systematic plans for using the information that was being collected in the facilities. A more recent project and relevant to the district was also described. This was a community wide information system project designed at the Provincial Medical Officer of health (PMO)'s office but had failed. In its conception, it was meant to be a success since *"we were sure we had personnel that can be trained, power in most facilities, information that would be fed to the system was available, existing procedures from the health records and information department work and even the district level managers received it very well. However, facilities and communities took too long to buy into the idea, when pushed they did not report all the details asked for, a problem of sensitization and poor knowledge on the importance of the simple information that they report on. The exercise called for major overhaul of data collection forms (tools) and organizational procedures – putting systems in place that would have supported the project."* One officer likened the project exercise to "climbing a tree from the branches" – whereas the project needed a systematic introduction synonymous with careful "climbing of the tree from the trunk" with all due preparation through involvement at all the stages. Preparation should have included educating the people to ensure they were aware of what they were being asked to do. The review of tools that was identified as needed also failed because the HMIS department that is mandated to make such changes had internal problems. Right from headquarters it was said to be headed by people who one participant described as being *"from the wrong profession, people who don't even know how to use computers."* The staffs at the dispensaries, health centers and hospitals had failed to receive the project well partly because for them it was an extra burden that meant more work that did not attract extra recognition.

It emerged that manual aggregation of data at the headquarters caused serious delays to the extent that even the three year reports from HMIS were published late. What was needed was a structure at the headquarters that would handle the submitted information (in electronic form). As it was, current information at the headquarters was not easily accessible when needed, necessitating repeated "urgent requests" that stretched the staff at the district and facility levels *"... sometimes not because the facility hasn't submitted, but because its cheaper to request another set than filter it from here. There is no information at the finger tips. One knows there is information out there, but has to collect, aggregate and summarize it every time it's needed. The enormously available information is not easily accessible. As it is, people get the realization when they have been asked."*

The health records and information department at headquarters was categorical that the policy of information collection and usage is that information should be used at the point of collection. *"It is not just for headquarters that information is collected but also the source is expected to use its bit"*. However this was not the case and a culture of acknowledging the role of information had not taken root in the sector. A complaint from the provincial office was that this is to the extent that the records department's staffs were sometimes not considered as part of the health services provision fraternity in the sector, budgeting allocation at the provincial levels rarely considered support for activities on data collection and reporting.

In a workshop with representatives from headquarters and district managers the response to the issues included informing the gathering that *"... there are ongoing review of tools through meetings with several development partners and NGOs – therefore the problems with the data collection tools are well known. It is just that the records people down here have no idea of what it means in the larger context. Concentration now is on building infrastructure, providing tools like computers."* On a positive note however, the meeting recognized "Hillside" as having been the first in the country to submit morbidity and mortality reports for 2003 and first quarter of 2004. The attitudes initially experienced in response to the ideas of the project were slowly changing and became very appreciative at policy level from those results. The prototype developed was found to be exemplary but it was noted that it was to be tested how far it was fitting in the ministry systems. With this positive reaction to the prototype, I attempted to present the grievances from the actual experiences of preparing the report (and the general problems encountered in data collection (including problems with the MoH 701 form). The reporting format from the ministry was quite rigid requiring detailing all the items to be included in the report, otherwise the report was not complete. I produced a list of diseases on the MoH 701 form excluding the ailments not occurring in the district but with additions that made the generalized categories on the official MoH 701 more specific (just as the clinical officers had suggested at the facility). My argument was that the ministry should allow printing of forms that were customized for the district to make the exercise more friendly and relevant. To my surprise this happened to be interpreted as equivalent to an insult. It was understood as failing to understand *"the way ministry works"* and to undermine the authority at headquarters. I was cautioned against imagining seeing what is seen in Europe *"... we are 100 years back, we can hop but not shorten 100 years to a day"*. The enthusiasm with which my prototype had been accepted was within an instance all gone. For the official at headquarters, the report was incomplete if it did not reflect the list of all diseases exactly as defined in the MoH 701 form. This incidence caused so much tension with the headquarters that eventually the project was unable to be established and the system developed beyond the "Hillside" prototype.

9. Appendix II: Project 2

Pre project

After I encountered problems that affected my continuity with the first project, I abruptly left the sector and returned to the University of Hamburg. The development agenda in the initial research plan was still burning and therefore, I continued looking for opportunities to make a contribution in the development of the health sector in Kenya. In collaboration with my supervisor, we looked for contacts of organizations working in the sector. The aim was to acquire a platform upon which I could make empirical experiences in the sector to further achieve my research objectives. One way of doing this was by getting direct funding for my proposal that I had revised so that it did not concentrate on the Hillside district only. Having failed to secure direct funding for the research project, I opted to take up an internship position with one donor agency working in the sector. My objectives were to form a basis upon which I collect empirical experiences.

Initial engagement with the donor agency involved advisory and development roles to the state-run national insurance organization. In the context of the engagement, I dealt and interacted with the senior ministry of health officials at the national level. It was upon completion of the automation of the quality assurance and accreditation process forms for hospitals that the donor agency retained me as an IT expert in charge of IT projects in its engagement with the ministry of health and other sector players. In this role, my interactions with the sector players, especially the MoH took a different look. I was considered an insider of the sector due to the fact that I had the donor agency's hat. This project, whose establishment process I describe here, was done in the context of the engagement with the donor agency.

Conceptualizing of the idea

The overall concept founding the project comes from the context of health reforms guided by the *Paris declaration on aid effectiveness* (WorldBank 2005). Senior ministers and heads of Governments met in Paris to review how effective the donor aid is. They came up with a declaration, signed by all the attendants, providing guidelines on how donor support in developing countries could be made more effective.

The thrust of the declaration was that countries receiving aid take the lead in the implementation and accompanying reforms. That meant a shift from the donor agencies implementing disjointed projects in various parts of the country into a single sector-wide strategic plan. For this, the host government takes the lead by defining its strategic objectives and identifying priorities then it presents them to all the sector players. As per the declaration, donors are expected to be partners in implementing the host country's defined priorities by aligning their aid to the set priorities within sector systems and procedures. This is what is known as Sector Wide Approach (SWAp) which means the donor interventions are harmonized and aligned to the developing country's sector structures, especially its strategic plans.

The Sector Wide Approach (SWAp) requires all partners on larger scale policy and project development efforts to place tremendous emphasis on the concept of partnership. SWAps are bound by the principles of all sector investments. Following an agreed Program of work; all partners in the SWAp arrangement agree on common management arrangements, funding for the implementation of the work Program channeled through government systems (central budget support as opposed to fragmented project funding); and lastly an existence of partnership agreements and working arrangements amongst the different partners. In the Kenyan Health Sector context, with the launch of the second National Health Sector Strategic Plan (NHSSPII) in 2005, several endeavors are already in place for a comprehensive Kenya Health SWAp.

In the bigger picture of ongoing sector reforms, the donors working in the Kenyan health sector established the "Health Donor Working Group" (HDWG). The donor agency I worked for is a key member of the working group. From the onset, consultations between the donors and government (as well as intra working group) were identified as a crucial aspect. A major element of the consultations are documents generated and shared internally within the working group, as well as documents that are generated by the group and shared with other sector stakeholders (including the ministry of health) for review. On the other hand, the process of getting documents by the donors from the government was found to be critical and faced problems of transparency and easy access. Specific need for timely access to such documents as sector strategies and guidelines needed to be addressed.

It is in this context that the project was conceived to develop a platform that facilitated easy sharing of documents among the HDWG members and with the ministry of health officials. The platform was conceptualized as a strategic resource that would increase transparency and facilitate easy sharing and access to such information resources in the reforms process. In the Health Donor Working Group, the platform was especially expected to simplify and facilitate better access to documents from the ministry. As a show of the seriousness with which the HDWG considered the problem of access to documents and support for collaboration, one member of the group from one of the United Nations health organizations drafted a simple demonstration (in the form of a web page). This was used as a proof of concept of how the members could leverage the internet to facilitate sharing of the information. In subsequent meetings, one donor agency took up the responsibility of funding the development of the platform by providing technical capacity, facilitating the process to come up with detailed requirements for the project and funding the resources needed to realize the platform. Moreover, for the donor agency, taking the lead in the development of the platform provided an opportunity to position itself as a key player in the reforms. The agency provided three experts, the head of the health division, me as the technical expert and an external consultant who brought prior experiences from the governance sector. The donor agency volunteered to take up the entire funding obligations in the development of the platform. It provided technical capacity, facilitated the process of coming up with detailed requirements for the project and funding the infrastructure needed to realize the platform. These were Web hosting, domain registration and maintenance and operations of the site.

Starting with the initial demonstration of drafted pages that had been generated; the concept was further developed to incorporate lessons from similar projects that had been done in Tanzania and Rwanda. These two countries already had working groups, with donors in the health sector having presence and so we borrowed ideas of what was involved.

Interactions with the working group
Highlights from the project process can be summarized as having involved among other tasks the following:
- Meeting with the developers of an initial concept
- Initial meeting in the regular monthly meetings of the HDWG
- Meeting with the ministry of health's representatives from the department overseeing reforms
- Series of meetings and sitting-in with the various programs – e.g. malaria, HIV and Aids
- Mini design workshop setting of the *"website reference group"* a small group formed from the HDWG as reference group in the project
- Presentation of progress and project status in the HDWG
- Series of consultations amongst the development partners and the government ministries

Highlights from the interactions: the case story
One of the very initial communications in the project was in the form of a mail that was a follow up from earlier informal discussions. I reproduce parts of it below (with attempts to remain anonymous as the persons and organizations involved).

```
Subject: HDWG
From: K****
Date: 2/1/2006 2:50 AM
To: H****
CC: M****, Salesio M. Kiura
Dear H****,

   Further to discussions with M**** yesterday, could we meet on the
HDWG web - site project. G**** (The donor agency) has some funds and
expertise, so we could assist to put it on-line.

Best regards, K****
```

Following discussions in the HDWG, further consultations were done bilaterally and this email was the formal commitment from the donor agency to further pursue the project. Following this, a meeting to review initial demonstration of concept was held. This review acted as a starting point during which the concept was extensively discussed. It was a successful meeting whereby the following highlights can be extracted (see exhibit above from an email)
- Formal confirmation of the start of the project process with description of how to get further mandate from the larger HDWG
- Handover of the initial developed proof of concept as the basis for further development
- Initial distribution of responsibilities such follow-up on technical details necessary for the project to go on
- Initial discussions on *modus operandi* in the project with decision reached such as establishment of a small subgroup of the HDWG to act as the reference group for the software development team. The small group to be essentially a part of the project team with provisions for discussions via emails or in meetings
- Discussions on the formalities necessary for the smooth running of the project such as the need to seek mandate from the larger group and the need to have formal terms of reference (TORs) that incorporates discussions from the meeting

```
From: G****
Sent: 01 February 2006 18:23
To: K****
Subject: Meeting mit UNICEF zu HDWG Homepage

Lieber k****,
das Meeting war konstruktiv. Wir haben das Verfahren mit H**** und
zwei IT Experten der UN besprochen und uns wurde das "Homepage
Skeleton" demonstriert, das UN**** für die HDWG erstellt hat. Dies
steckt noch in den Kinderschuhen, ist jedoch eine gute
Entwicklungsbasis. Salasio hat eine Kopie mitgenommen und wird dir
über die technischen Daten berichten können. Ich bat ihn auch darum,
Fragen und technische Herausforderungen zu benennen, über die die
HDWG bald entscheiden muß (z.B. welcher Server, welche soft ware,
Abstimmung über die Regularien und Sicherheitsbestimmungen der
beteiligten Geber etc.).

Mit Heimo sind wir übereingekommen, dass wir bei der nächsten HDWG
offiziell um Mandatserteilung bitten, um das Projekt fortzuführen.
Die G**** (Du oder ich?) sollte dies mit M**** vorab klären und auf
die Agenda bringen. Dann ist es sicher gut, wenn sich eine
Untergruppe der HDWG gründet, die als Referenzgruppe für die GTZ und
Salassio zur Verfügung steht, wenn technische und rechtliche (?)
Dinge abgeklärt werden müssen. Diese Gruppe sollte sich auch ad hoc
treffen können oder per mail austauschen. H**** hat seine Teilnahme
zugesichert. ... Auch sollte sich jemand bereit erklären, die Oberaufsicht zu übernehmen. Dann ist noch die
Frage der Langzeitfinanzierung und
Pflege zu klären. Auch sollte geklärt werde, wer die Page "hosted"
und wie lange. All diese Punkte werden auch auf die ToRs der HDWG
einwirken, aber die wollten wir ja sowieso überarbeiten.

Wir kamen abschließend überein, mit der Entwicklung der HDWG homepage
zügig anzufangen ...

Soweit in Kürze und nun mach ich meinen Mac aus

G****
```

Parallel to the engagements with the HDWG, I also had engagements with the ministry of health through a meeting with the department responsible for reforms. The head of the donor agency and the head of the department had informal consultations that were followed by an invitation for a meeting as described in the email exhibit below.

```
From: K****
Sent: 01 February 2006 18:23
To: Salesio M. Kiura
Subject: FW: DEVELOPMENT OF AN INFORMATION SYSTEM


T**** (Head of department) has told me she is ready for a meeting. Pls.
prepare a presentation for that with a easy to read list of questions
and decisions as well as a model for the different options which we can
use for demonstration.
```

> Will discuss more today.
>
> Best regards, K****
> ----
> From: S**** @****moh.go.ke]
> Sent: 20 January 2006 07:38
> To: K****
> Subject: Re: DEVELOPMENT OF AN INFORMATION SYSTEM
>
> Dear K****,
> We accept the earlier submitted document on the above. Attached please find our brief.
> T*****

The meeting was held where we clarified on the need for a communication platform. Here the various resources available from the department would be made easily accessible to among others the donor community. MoH's response was positive, and at length expounded on their mandate especially on coordination of tasks dealing with the donors. The representatives immediately pointed out the fact that HSRS is the nerve center of the ministry reform activities. On being called upon to expound the meaning of this, the response from the group can be summarized as having touched on:
- the department understands itself as the custodian of the documents that guide the operations of the ministry at all levels
- the department facilitates development of policies through tasks that cut across various other departments
- as coordinating unit, the department advices on ongoing projects and interventions in the sector
- the wide spectrum of the consumers of the department's services is testimony of the central role the department plays. These include: ministry of health departments, provincial and district offices, other arms of the government, the general public, international organizations and also the private sector.

In response to the problem of communication from a donor's perspective, the department was on the offensive, citing political interests from different donors and the failure to recognize the importance of the department in the reforms agenda. Previous endeavors aimed at enhancing communication from the ministry were described. The reasons attributed for these failures were stated as problems in getting stakeholders to agree and lack of forums from which stakeholders can easily communicate and share their practices.

For the project to continue, it was however explained that the ministry was undergoing reforms that would affect the operations of the department as part of the sector. The department's place in the sector would probably change together with the services, especially supervisory roles that it plays. A senior Programme officer said it was necessary that we consult the head of the department and other higher offices in the ministry. *With the drastic changes spelt out in the international declarations of how to operate reforms in the country a communication office for liaising with donors is necessary.* The argument was that the department was not ready for a document management system or a website. It was necessary at this point to get past this state of affairs. A reassurance and production of emails ascertaining that the head of the department had directed we proceed, that the structure in place was enough for the department staff to collaborate in the project. Another point of discussion arose concerning the suitability of the department as the direct partner in the project. This pointed at power issues across departments and programs at the ministry's top hierarchy. A line of thought followed was that there are specific departments and programs that specialize on specific thematic areas such as malaria, HIV and AIDS, child health, etc. From these programs the respective documents are produced and published. Therefore they are better placed to provide the current documents than the reforms department which has supervisory roles in the process of the documents generation. This expanded the projects team to include representatives from these programs albeit not in the core project team. As a consequence, we had meetings with the heads of the programs that corresponded with the inter agency coordination committees from the HDWG (Child health, health systems, HIV and AIDS, Malaria, reproductive health, Tuberculosis). These were helpful in the initial definition of understanding the sector.

Further to this, we had meetings with the HDWG. It was important that we have the agenda included in the meeting. This was to ensure that the initiative was received as coming from the chair and not from a single donor agency summoning the others. As deciphered from the exhibit email below, there are undercurrents of power issues also amongst the donors. It was necessary that other donor agencies are given recognition. As can be seen from the start of the conversation, the aspect of informal consultations and deliberations in the background is very strong. The communication is only formalized through an email after there have already been negotiations and discussions that have lead to an agreement in one way or another (cf. about the project getting a slot for the presentation and about the meeting agenda).

```
-----Original Message-----
From: R**** - Donor agency II
Sent: 16 February 2006 10:28
To: G****
Cc: K****; M****
Subject: SV: Health Donor Working Group Meeting, 22nd Feb 2006

Dear G****,
Thanks for your mail. Is it possible to shorten the presentation
perhaps to 10 minutes and leave 5 minutes for questions. The meeting is
scheduled to end at 11.30 and there will be two more short
presentations by other partners. Would be glad if this is possible.

Best regards
R****

-----Original Message-----
From: G****
Sent: 14 February 2006 15:24
To: R****
Cc: K****
Subject: Re: Health Donor Working Group Meeting, 22nd Feb 2006

Dear R****,
thank you for sending me the draft agenda for the next HDWG meeting.
We will give a powerpoint presentation which will take apprx. 25 min
(incl. questions). Kindly provide the beamer.

Thank you and best regards
G****

On 15.02.2006, at 11:41, Rhodah Wanjiku Njuguna wrote:
> > <Health Donor Working Group Meeting 22nd Feb 2006.doc>

From: G****
Sent: 01 February 2006 18:23
To: Salesio M. Kiura; K****
Subject: FW: DEVELOPMENT OF AN INFORMATION SYSTEM

Dear Salesio and ****,
just spoke to M****. The next HDWG meeting is set for Wednesday, 22
February at 9.30 a.m. We will have a slot for our presentation on the
website. I arranged for a beamer. Salesio, we will go through your
draft tomorrow and discuss the presentation in detail. Thanks, I
received your draft.

Best
G****
```

To further exhibit the informality with which the project was done, the email exhibit below shows that even the intra project group, informal meetings in environments outside the work offices were also done. These helped build a better understanding of the mindset of the audience in the meetings. Through informal preparatory meetings akin to coaching each other, incorporation of audience's interests is guaranteed.

> Subject: Re: HDWG presentation/meeting tomorrow
> From: G****
> To: Salesio M.Kiura
> CC: K****
>
> Hallo Salesio,
> wie besprochen treffen wir (K****, Du und ich) uns heute Abend um 6 Uhr bei mir.
> Bis dann
> G****

We had a presentation in the HDWG meeting where we successfully got the official mandate to proceed. More members joined the website reference group for further inputs. Moreover we were able to present and answer questions regarding such issues as the feasibility of the project, the experiences from other development partner groups in the region, agreement on the management of the project, the clarification of the contents and design as well as an initial presentation of our advice concerning the technical requirements for the project. A set of basic features for a collaboration platform in the sector was also presented as entailing: thematic representation of the organization, a shared calendar, up-to-date news and events, download/upload of documents and publications, inclusiveness (registration, dates to note), discussion forums.

Features in the new design that presented additional functionalities were also presented. The technical options for the development of the platform were also discussed and a timeframe agreed upon. The important thing from this was that the whole group had the opportunity to discuss the project options to greater details that enabled the members get involved in the project. This was symbolized by the number that volunteered for the web site reference group.

As a follow up, I had meetings with specific thematic groups where we deliberated on the contents and design of the relevant pages that hold information about their working themes. The meetings took place in their offices and were preceded by telephone conversations that explained the expectation from the meetings, the kind of resources expected from the meetings – e.g. set of relevant documents describing the thematic groups. These engagements that involved spending time with the officers responsible, assisting them in their immediate tasks and where necessary extending the support to the officers beyond the project.

In another follow up meeting with the reforms department, it was agreed that there was need of a formal commitment in the form of a memorandum of understanding to be signed between the donor agency and the government department. As a preparation for the meeting, I met the technical person in a workshop setting in which a detailed design of the platform in the form of a navigation structure and normalized data base. In this setting, we identified the relevant information and technical recommendations to be made to the larger group of the project. There were problems concerning the ease with which the ministry officers could do their research on topic relevant to the identified technical problems. They were limited by the available infrastructure; there were gaps with keeping abreast with technological developments as to information about relevant technologies for web development, etc. With the idea that I could meet the technical and professional staff independently I was able to have them research on areas from which they were required to provide inputs on. However, it's worth mentioning that when it came to the technical and professional staffs providing inputs in meetings, there were several meetings cancellations and altered agendas. When a meeting was canceled, what followed was a small team meeting that discussed the issues into details and negotiated a compromise position. Sometimes the agendas proposed for meetings could be changed abruptly by way of additions of new agenda items without prior warning. This sometimes caused a lot of strain on the external consultants in the project. Other times, the agenda items were slashed off the list citing – "still following up in that" or that there were consultation with the head of the ICT in the ministry or the head of the department has not responded.

> ...
> Wir kamen abschließend überein, mit der Entwicklung der HDWG Homepage zügig anzufangen und nicht auf das MoH zu warten. Man kann zu einem späteren Zeitpunkt beide Websites ohne Schwierigkeiten verknüpfen.
> ...

This was to the extent that the HDWG realized the ministry was lagging behind in the project and decided that the ministry was to have its own platform and link up later the two sites: one from the donor working group and the other from the reforms department (see exhibit email above).

The background to the drastic decision can be summarized as a difference in pace of working between the development partners and the government departments. The government department requested for inclusion in the project engagement:
- support in setting up of a network infrastructure at the department,
- provision of laptops to government officers in the project
- provision of sitting allowances to the officers for participating in the project meetings
- provision of web authoring tools and training of the ICT officers

To cater for these, it needed preparation of a memorandum of understanding (MoU) between the donor agency and the reforms department. This process was to take long and therefore a decision was reached to proceed with the development of the projects independent of each other. The project was successfully established and the results are online to date.

10. Appendix III: Project 3

Platform for storing and sharing results from the technical working group on collaboration between the public and faith-based health service providers

Overview:

This is a project whose establishment took a relatively faster pace to establish because of experiences drawn from the earlier projects and other projects whose results are not directly reported in this study. These include establishment and development of weblogs (e.g. for the donor agency's health division and for sharing experiences during the establishment of the Kenya Health SWAp process), the development of a website for an umbrella organization representing all health NGOs working in Kenya as well as a platform to support a taskforce reviewing health care financing mechanisms. I select to report on the project with the technical working group on collaboration between the public and faith based health services providers since it represents a relatively smoother and faster process irrespective of the representations from diverse organizations. The representatives were selected from public and private health services providers as well as from the donor communities.

The overall goal of the project comes from the context of Sector wide Approaches (SWAps). The aim is to establish instruments of implementing the Paris declaration on aid effectiveness and accelerating achievement of health related Millennium Development Goals (MDGS) (UN Website) through exchange of synergies between all players in the health sector. To achieve such synergies, the engagement of the civil society as partners with the public sector is necessary. The health related civil society organizations play a major role in the provision of health services in Kenya. By recognizing them as key partners of the public health ministry, a Technical Working Group (TWG) was formed to formalize the partnership. An observation from the technical working group was that there had been other efforts to establish partnership between the public and the civil society as early as 1984. About ten years later, they were starting the process from scratch without any documentation from previous endeavors. A part of the objective for the platform was therefore set to provide a living memory of the work of the working group. It was also aimed at enabling easy sharing of the results from the group to the members through a means of centrally exchanging documents, announcements and a common shared calendar of events.

Highlights

The donor agency I was working for had by now strongly established itself as a champion of information dissemination in the sector. Armed with the objective of sharing experiences beyond the public sector structures, the donor agency took up responsibility of facilitating the development of a platform upon which collaboration between the members of the technical working group could be enhanced. The process formally started with a workshop of the selected working by having a retreat on the outskirts of Nairobi. Whereas there had been discussions with the individual technical working group member organizations, it was at this workshop that all previous findings from discussions were consolidated. As a representative of the donor agency I facilitated a half day workshop. This was an intensive process during which a smaller group from the technical working group was not only selected but also a chair and a secretary were selected. The participants freely engaged in detailed discussions and consensus was used to thrush out differences. For example to ensure ownership, a rotating mechanism of the chair and secretary to the group was defined. This was designed to give the six represented organizations a chance to hold these positions. These were the Protestants, Catholics, Muslims, suppliers of essential drugs and equipments and the ministry of health. The development partners were defined as facilitating observers to the process.

I represented aggregated summary of features identified in the previous meetings with individual members of the organizations. Whereas there were no disagreements about the features, a disagreement on the prioritization of the features arose and this was through shared graphical representation discussed and a compromise arrived at. Another aspect was the workflow process for publishing documents. Even though it was not conclusively settled in the workshop, decisions were made to enable an initial start of development. Further consultations discussed the process as it developed from use of the prototypes before the final launch of the site.

Another major and relevant incidence in the project's initial stages is what we termed as a "dissemination seminar" where preliminary results from the project were demonstrated. Rather than I (representing the donor agency) being the convener of the meetings, the working group's chair was the host. As the email excerpt exhibit below shows, the visits I had to the member institutions had included interactions that were beyond the limited scope of the project. The limited stays with the departments' heads had included processes that lead to them building insights to ICT opportunities to support their processes. The newly earned knowledge had lead to visions about the possibilities for having specialized systems to support their processes.

```
From: gs@C****
Sent: 19 September 2006 10:23
To: undisclosed-recipients
cc: Salesio M. Kiura
Subject: Invitation to Seminar

Dear Colleagues,

I have the pleasure to invite you to a one day workshop at C****
offices on 30th September 2006 starting at 9:00AM. During this seminar
we are going to disseminate the results from an ongoing project in
support of the technical working group on MOH-FBHS collaboration.

Mr. Salesio Mbogo from G**** will take us through the preliminary
results of the website for the technical working group. Moreover, we
will have the opportunity to review the results and their implications
for how our member organizations work.

To move further the new insights his interactions has developed during
his stays at our ICT departments, we have in the agenda a session to
explore opportunities for standardized applicable solutions for our
member organizations

Best regards, M****
Secretary, MoH-FBHS-TWG
```

Die VDM Verlagsservicegesellschaft sucht für wissenschaftliche Verlage abgeschlossene und herausragende

Dissertationen, Habilitationen, Diplomarbeiten, Master Theses, Magisterarbeiten usw.

für die kostenlose Publikation als Fachbuch.

Sie verfügen über eine Arbeit, die hohen inhaltlichen und formalen Ansprüchen genügt, und haben Interesse an einer honorarvergüteten Publikation?

Dann senden Sie bitte erste Informationen über sich und Ihre Arbeit per Email an *info@vdm-vsg.de*.

Sie erhalten kurzfristig unser Feedback!

VDM Verlagsservicegesellschaft mbH
Dudweiler Landstr. 99 Telefon +49 681 3720 174
D - 66123 Saarbrücken Fax   +49 681 3720 1749
www.vdm-vsg.de

Die VDM Verlagsservicegesellschaft mbH vertritt

Printed by Books on Demand GmbH, Norderstedt / Germany